Dreams and Dreaming

Dreams and Dreaming

By the Editors of Time-Life Books

TIME-LIFE BOOKS, ALEXANDRIA, VIRGINIA

CONTENTS

The trancelike stillness, silvery light, and empty landscape of Henri Rousseau's 1897 painting The Sleeping Gypsy are expressive of the mood as well as the setting of a haunting dream.

The World of the Inner Eye

The moonlit desert of *The Sleeping Gypsy (left),* where a woman slumbers oblivious to the menacing lion behind her, evokes the magical world of a dream. In works such as this, French artist Henri Rousseau foreshadowed the early-twentieth-century literary and artistic movement that was to hold the dream omnipotent—surrealism.

Artists have always been interested in dreams, but the surrealists, heavily influenced by the work of psychoanalyst Sigmund Freud, were the first to approach painting as a way of investigating dreams and the subconscious rather than as an end in itself. Accordingly, they sought to transcend the world of conscious thought, or reality, by depicting unaltered the images seen by the inner eye, the subconscious vision, they believed, through which we experience dreams. The self-appointed spokesman of surrealism, French poet André Breton, declared the goal as "the future resolution of these two states, so contradictory in appearance—dream and reality—into a kind of absolute reality, or surreality."

To realize this aim in pictorial form, the artists used common dream elements. Ordinary objects are distorted or juxtaposed in extraordinary ways and may take on symbolic meaning. Events of the past, present, and future may all be taking place at once. And the laws that govern physical reality are suspended. The following portfolio offers visual entryway into the realm that is the subject of this book—the fascinating world of dreams and dreaming.

The Exotic Reveries of Henri Rousseau

Although French painter Henri Rousseau never set foot in a jungle, tropical forests grew deep and lush in the fertile ground of his imagination. Indeed, the self-taught artist rarely left Paris, but he frequented the botanical and zoological gardens that were there, gathering inspiration for his evocative images. "When I enter these hothouses and see these strange plants from exotic countries," Rousseau once remarked, "I feel as if I have stepped into a dream."

The sensation of entering a dream strikes many who view Rousseau's works of art, particularly the large painting aptly titled *The Dream (right)*. The canvas features a nude woman reclining on a couch amid the verdant foliage of a moonlit jungle; a snake charmer and wild animals lurk close at hand.

In a letter to an inquiring art critic, Rousseau once gave an explanation for the incongruities of the image. "The woman asleep on the couch is dreaming she has been transported into the forest," the artist commented. She remains at home, traveling in dreams to a world that is beyond reach. Similarly, Rousseau himself was carried by his inner vision far beyond the confines of his Paris studio to the alluring dreamscapes he so lovingly transferred to canvas.

The Dream, 1910

Marc Chagall's Lyric Visions

When pressed to explain why he became a painter, Marc Chagall responded that painting "seemed to me like a window through which I could have taken flight toward another world." And another world—a magical place where the mundane mingles with the fantastic—is just what his works portray.

In *The Yellow Room (right),* for instance, the table is set for tea, a common enough scene. The perspective, however, is anything but common. The table appears so tilted that in waking life the cups and samovar could slide off. And the diners, one of whom is a cow, are hardly ordinary: The woman's head is on upside down and the man is faceless. Indeed, the whole setting evokes the kind of crazy dream that challenges the very definition of reality.

In blurring the bounds between the real and the unreal, Chagall had much in common with the surrealists, although he never considered himself a member of the movement. "Our whole inner world is reality," he wrote, "perhaps more real still than the apparent world."

Chagall's "apparent" world was Paris, where he lived most of his adult life. At least part of his inner world, however, belonged to the Russian village of Vitebsk, where he was born in 1887 and

The Yellow Room, 1911

Fantastic Horse Cart, 1949

where he spent his youth. Memories of that village—the people, the architecture, the animals—embellished by his imagination and placed in absurd situations, fill his canvases.

In *Fantastic Horse Cart (below)*, an enormous green horse carries a huge, blue-faced fiddler down a seemingly ordinary village street; the passengers in the cart appear unconcerned by his cavorting. And in *The Juggler (right)*, a high-kicking birdlike creature commands center stage in a circus. The tiny fiddler, the clock, the

horses, the spectators, and all the other elements in the painting contribute to the dreamlike confusion. In fact, some of those objects are common dream symbols. Clocks are obvious representations of time and change. Horses, in some circumstances, may indicate passion or sexual energy, and so on—but Chagall downplayed their importance. "I work with no express symbols but as it were subconsciously," he said. "When the picture is finished everyone can interpret it as he wishes."

The Entombment, 1957

Frozen Fragments of Delvaux's Dreams

The paintings of twentieth-century Belgian artist Paul Delvaux often seem to capture a fleeting moment in a haunting dream, as if the artist had taken mental snapshots of subconscious scenes and transferred them to canvas. Pervasive in Delvaux's work is a reverberating stillness—the figures appear to move as if in sleep, rarely taking notice of the viewer or of one another.

Frequently the pictures assume classical overtones, and elements from disparate time periods are often juxtaposed. In *Penelope (left),* an ancient temple coexists with what appears to be a train station, also a recurring image in Delvaux's work. On the station's platform, an elegantly

robed woman and the two nudes behind her reveal no bond between them. Yet the three women seem to be linked by silence, which Delvaux referred to as his "way of expressing the climate, the mystery of things."

Another favorite theme of Delvaux's—skeletons—is featured in *The Entombment (above).* A dream symbol that may represent illness or misunderstanding, skeletons frequently appeared in works by the surrealists, with whom the artist is often grouped. In contrast to his somnambulistic humans, Delvaux's corpses seem to come alive. For him, skeletons represented not death but "the framework of the human being, the living creature."

The Unmasked Universe, date unknown

René Magritte, the Deliberate Dreamer

"Painting," wrote artist René Magritte, "reveals images of the world, and it can happen that in looking at them, painting them, thinking about them, we have this unfamiliar feeling of our mystery—one we also have sometimes with our eyes closed." In works such as *Polar Light (right)*, Magritte—a compatriot and contemporary of Paul Delvaux—succeeds in capturing the startling, dreamlike mystery of which he spoke.

In the painting, a curious, birdlike object shares the foreground with two hollow, female forms, whose fragile shells appear to have been pecked away in great chunks. The group's silence is echoed in the painting's still, barren landscape, with its peculiar peaks and its ominous skies.

Although this particular work suggests a highly symbolic dream, Magritte denied that the objects he painted were symbols of any kind. He considered his pictures to be "material tokens of the freedom of thought." Indeed, Magritte discounted the importance of nocturnal images in the creative process. "If we deal with dreams," he wrote, "they are very different from the dreams we have when asleep. These are very voluntary dreams with none of the vagueness of feeling we have when escaping into dream." Nonetheless, as a mature artist, Magritte stressed the importance of the ideas that came to him in the so-called hypnagogic state, the drowsy period we experience just before waking or while falling asleep. And the committed surrealist defined the movement as demanding "for our waking lives a liberty comparable to that that we possess in dreams."

Many of Magritte's paintings contain common dream symbols. The house, for instance, is often thought to represent a person's body or whole personality. In *The Unmasked Universe (above)*, the structure is an empty shell shored up by beams and scaffolds. Whether the scene is one of construction or destruction, if either, is open to debate, thereby reflecting Magritte's intention to "paint only images that evoke the world's mystery."

Polar Light, 1927

Shades of Night Descending, 1931

Perspectives, 1939

Salvador Dali's Simulated Madness

Although most surrealist artists were influenced to one degree or another by Sigmund Freud's theories of dreams and the subconscious, none embraced his ideas so fervently as did Spanish painter Salvador Dali. Freud's *The Interpretation of Dreams* seemed to Dali a revelation, since for him it represented a scientific explanation for the torments and erotic fantasies he claimed to have experienced ever since childhood. His subsequent fascination with psychoanalysis at once affected his approach to his art.

But while most surrealists depicted the images from the subconscious—which Freud had defined as uncontrolled by conscious reason—in more or less lyric terms, Dali wanted to document them with scientific accuracy. He proposed to do this not by merely retrieving images

from his subconscious mind but by controlling them through his idiosyncratic "paranoiac-critical method."

Simply put, he simulated madness, or paranoia, in order to obtain and depict an image from his subconscious. Then, through a deliberate Freudian process of free association, he added to the painting any other images suggested by the initial form. Rendering the results with masterful attention to detail, Dali created dream worlds that seem as tangibly real as everyday existence.

The finely drawn rock formations in *Shades of Night Descending (left)*, for instance, lend an air of hard reality to the flat, ominous landscape menaced by dense shadows. And in *Perspectives (above)*, the barren desert, phantasmagorical sky, and contorted, tortured-looking

Sleep, 1937

humans combine to create a chillingly vivid nightmare.

Throughout his long career, Dali was fascinated by the idea of the double image, one that suggests or turns into a second image—a common occurrence in dreams. The enormous head depicted in *Sleep (left)* is an example of such a device. At first glance it seems merely a monstrous, balloonlike visage. But upon further examination, the image begins to resemble a fetus.

Art historian James Thrall Soby explained in his 1941 book, *Salvador Dali,* that for Dali, sleep was paradoxical. It was a monster, "because in their dreams, men are free to commit the most hideous crimes; sleep was embryonic, because it gives men the warm shelter and immunity of the womb."

The artist himself—who died at the age of eighty-four in 1989—reportedly said the crutches in the painting symbolize what he termed the "psychic balance" that makes sleep possible. Taking just one away, according to Dali's cryptic explanation, would result in insomnia.

CHAPTER 1

Where Reality Meets Illusion

nce upon a time Chuang Chou dreamt he was a butterfly, a butterfly flitting and fluttering around, happy with himself and doing as he pleased. Suddenly he woke up and there he was, solid and unmistakable Chuang Chou. But he didn't know if he was Chuang Chou who had dreamt he was a butterfly, or a butterfly dreaming he was Chuang Chou.''

The blurring between waking consciousness and the world we enter only when we sleep is a theme that runs throughout the graceful and imaginative writings of Chuang Chou, a highly respected fourth-century-BC Chinese philosopher also known as Chuang-tzu—Master Chuang. In fact, the distinction between reality and dreams has captivated humankind in all ages. Some peoples believed—and some still do believe—that dreams are as real as any waking event. And many of us can recall times when we have awakened from a vivid dream confused and disoriented, unsure of which landscape we actually inhabit, the room we see around us or the nighttime vision still lingering in our heads.

Dreaming is a universal and powerful experience—all humans sleep, and all humans dream. Dreams can be fleeting fragments of images or entire complicated narratives unreeling like movies before the mind's eye. The visions can appear benign or soothing, or they can inspire heart-pounding terror. They can be peopled with friends and loved ones or commanded by horrifying monsters. Dreams can mimic reality or create a totally surreal environment. They can be clear and detailed or jumbled and confused. They may impart wisdom or knowledge, or they may leave the dreamer completely baffled by their content.

But even when all those frequently experienced characteristics of dreams are acknowledged, there remain many puzzling questions about the familiar phenomenon: What are dreams? Where do they come from? And what significance, if any, do they hold for the dreamer's life? The variety of answers set forth to these questions over time reflects the values and the social and psychological structures of various cultures. Ancient peoples, among them the Egyptians and the Greeks, believed dreams were messages sent by the gods to sleeping minds. The father of modern psychiatry, Sigmund Freud, thought that dreams, created by the human brain, could serve as windows into the psyche, revealing a cache of wishes unfulfilled, and many of his followers today consider such visions to be a major tool in psychoanalysis. On the other hand, some scientists have theorized that dreams are unnecessary bits of information being expunged nightly from a person's memory, just as a computer's files are cleaned of unwanted data. And researchers into the paranormal, in some ways echoing the ancients, believe dreams may have a psychic element, revealing the forces of destiny, the reality that is about to happen.

Whatever their beliefs, humans have always searched for the meanings of dreams, the logic hidden beneath layers of symbolism and metaphor: In the Hebrew Talmud, it is written, "A dream not interpreted is like a letter to the self unread." The ancients drew up elaborate dream books, listing common dreams and their meanings, and respected dream interpreters did a brisk business. Today, seekers examine their dreams from an analyst's couch or by sharing them with a group in what are called "dreamwork" therapy sessions. Some enthusiasts suggest that we can understand the real world only by unlocking the secrets of our dreams. They point out that many of history's most influential individuals—Alexander the Great, René Descartes, Elias Howe, and Robert Louis Stevenson, to name but a few—claimed to have been directed by their dreams. Others contend that nocturnal images are our passport into another dimension, a whole other reality.

But to many philosophers, the central question of dreams is expressed by Chuang Chou's butterfly paradox. Many thinkers of the ancient East joined him in considering where lies the line of demarcation between dreams and reality and which side of the line we are on at any given time. Like Chuang Chou, these writers suggested that one cannot judge whether dreams or waking experiences are the more real. One such author was Li Yuan chuo, a professor at China's renowned Imperial Academy during the Southern Song dynasty, which flourished during the twelfth and thirteenth centuries. In an essay on the butterfly dream, Li argued that since the states of dreaming and waking consciousness coexist within the same being, there must be some point of contact between the two. However, he continued, to the extent that each state constitutes a world of its own, one is as real—and as false—as the other. "Since in dream one is not aware of the wakeful state, the dream is not taken to be delusive," Li wrote. "Likewise, while awake, one does not know about the dream state, hence wakefulness is not regarded as real."

Ancient Chinese literature is replete with references to dreams and how they relate to conscious existence. The Buddhists considered dreams to be part and parcel of reality. In a work dating from the Ming dynasty, which ruled from 1368 to 1644, an author named Lian chi Ba shi wrote, "The old saying goes: Living in this world is like having a big dream. And Scripture says: When we come to look at the world, it is comparable to things in a dream." Feng Meng long, a novelist of the seventeenth century, presented the dream versus reality debate from a more earthy perspective. "A great drinker dreamed that he possessed some good wine," Feng related in his book entitled *Hsiao-fu* (House of Laughter). "He was about to heat and drink it

The fragment of old sculpture at right depicts Hypnos, the ancient
Greek god of sleep. Hypnos was believed to be the brother of figures who appeared
in dreams, and his son Morpheus was the god of dreams.

when he suddenly woke up. Remorseful, he said, 'I should have taken it cold!'"

This blending of illusion and reality also plays an important role in many of the great Hindu myths. One story, the tale of Krishna (an incarnation of the god Vishnu) and Yasoda (Krishna's mortal mother), opens with Krishna being scolded for having eaten dirt. "But I haven't," explains young Krishna. "All the boys are lying; . . . look at my mouth." "Then open up," says Yasoda to the god who had taken the form of a human child. When he obliged, "she saw in his mouth the whole universe, with the far corners of the sky, and the wind, and lightning, and the orb of the earth with its mountains and oceans, and the moon and stars, and space itself; and she saw her own village and herself. She became frightened and confused, thinking, 'Is this a dream or an illusion fabricated by God? Or is it a delusion in my own mind?'" Yasoda questioned which was her true existence—that which she had always considered reality or the second universe glimpsed inside her young son's mouth in her dreamlike experience.

The debate between reality and illusion was not limited to Eastern thinkers. Some classical Greek philosophers addressed the same point. In Plato's *Theaetetus,* Socrates asks, "What proof could you give if anyone should ask us now, at the present moment, whether we are asleep and our thoughts are a dream, or whether we are awake and talking with each other in a waking condition?" After Theaetetus admits they could both be dreaming, Socrates continues, "So you see, it is even open to dispute whether we are awake or in a dream."

ven psychoanalyst Carl Jung, who followed his mentor Sigmund Freud in pursuing the significance of dreams to psychological well-being, on at least one occasion found himself caught in his own version of the butterfly paradox. In his 1963 autobiography, *Memories, Dreams, Reflections,* Jung recounted a dream he had in 1944, after a long illness. "I was walking along a little road through a hilly landscape. . . . Then I came to a small wayside chapel. The door was ajar, and I

went in. . . . In front of the altar, facing me, sat a yogi—in lotus posture in deep meditation. When I looked at him more closely, I realized that he had my face. I stared in profound surprise, and awoke with the thought: 'Aha, so he is the one who is meditating me. He has a dream and I am it.'"

In some cultures, the philosophical debate between reality and dreams has no relevance whatsoever—since those cultures draw no distinction between the world of dreams and real life. Consider the case of the African chief who dreamed he had visited England and Portugal. When he awoke he dressed in Western clothes and described his trip to his people. They greeted him and congratulated him on his safe "journey."

The Kai tribe of New Guinea and the West African Ashantis also equate dreams with reality. They believe that if a man dreams of committing adultery, he must be punished. The Pokomam peoples of Guatemala and many other tribes claim that the dreamer's soul leaves the body at night

and that its actions are then recorded in dreams. Africa's Zulu peoples contend it is through their dreams that ancestral spirits evaluate the actions of the living and register their approval or dismay. And among the San people of the Kalahari Desert in southern Africa, the butterfly paradox would be no paradox at all. When British writer Laurens van der Post asked some of them to talk about their dreams, a San elder told him, "But you see, it is very difficult, for always there is a dream dreaming us."

For most Western people, the question at the root of the butterfly paradox is merely a philosophical exercise; they recognize the distinction between dream and reality. Much more pressing is the issue of what a particular dream means. The desire to interpret dreams, to discover their underlying significance or message for action, cuts across cultural boundaries—although the meanings ascribed to the same dream images can vary greatly from people to people. For example, the Quiche Maya in the highlands of Guatemala and the Zuni Indians of New Mexico share a deep respect for their ancestors. However, if a Zuni dreams of an ancestor, he invariably describes it as a harrowing experience and must seek a cure via a religious ritual—while if a Quiche dreams of a dead forebear, it is seen as a positive event, a cause for rejoicing. After such a dream a Quiche invariably visits one of the tribe's "daykeepers," or dream interpreters, to have the dream analyzed. Quiche daykeepers, both male and female, are trained from an early age in the intricacies of dream interpretation.

Interest in dream interpretation, especially the attempt to predict the future by analyzing dreams, spans eras as well as cultures. Many centuries before Chuang Chou wrote on the subject, the ancient Egyptians became fascinated with unlocking the meaning of their dreams. They are credited with establishing the science of oneiromancy, or dream divination, as expressed in the engraved tablet that served as a "calling card" for an ancient Egyptian dream interpreter: "I interpret dreams, having the gods' mandate to do so."

Other clues to the Egyptians' techniques of dream interpretation include an Egyptian text attributed to King Merikare, a pharaoh who ruled about 2070 BC. In the text Merikare describes dreams as an intuition of a possible future. The pharaoh apparently believed that dreams symbolized exactly the opposite of what they seemed to; visions of happiness, for example, foretold imminent disaster. Another fragment of text dates from sometime during the Middle Kingdom period—between 2000 BC and 1785 BC—and features a list of nearly 200 traditional dream interpretations used in divination:

"If a man sees himself in a dream looking at a dead ox it is good, since it signifies the death of his enemies.

"If a man sees in a dream his bed on fire it is bad, since it signifies the rape of his wife.

"If a man sees himself in a dream looking at a snake it is good, since it signifies an abundance of provisions."

For the Egyptians, then, dreams were a way of seeing into some deeper reality, a belief shared by their neighbors the Israelites, whose words for "to dream" and "to see" were the same. The Israelites believed dreams to be messages from God, and they relied on patriarchs such as Joseph and Daniel to interpret them. Joseph's story is one of the earliest—and best-known—cases of dream divination. According to the book of Genesis, Joseph, son of Jacob, related to his brothers a dream in which "we were binding sheaves in the field, and lo, my sheaf arose and stood upright; and behold, your sheaves gathered around it, and bowed down to my sheaf; . . . behold, the sun, moon, and eleven stars were bowing down to me." Deciding that he should be punished, his eleven brothers kidnapped Joseph and sold him into slavery in Egypt.

In his Egyptian prison, he met two inmates, the pharaoh's butler and baker. "And Joseph saw them in the morning and they were sad and he asked, 'whereof look ye so sad today?' And they told him, 'We dreamed a dream and there was no interpreter.' And Joseph said to them, 'Do not interpretations belong to God? Tell me them, I pray you.' "

Joseph listened to the prisoners' dreams and, demon-

夢齎良弼

strating the power God had given him, explained the meanings of their visions—the butler would be freed from prison and be back in the pharaoh's service within three days, but the baker would be hanged for his crime. Sure enough, according to the Bible, "all this came to pass."

Joseph languished in prison for another two years until he was summoned, on the recommendation of the butler, to help interpret a dream that had troubled the pharaoh and confounded his wise men. The pharaoh said that in his dream he had stood on the bank of the Nile and watched "seven fat kine" (cows) come up out of the river. As the fat cows grazed, he said, "seven other kine followed them; poor and very ill-favored and lean-fleshed, much as I had never seen in Egypt. And the ill-famed kine did eat up the fat kine." The pharaoh had awakened, but later the dream

continued, showing him seven full heads of grain being devoured by seven withered heads of grain.

Joseph told the pharaoh his dream was a warning from God to the Egyptians that they would enjoy seven years of plenty, followed by seven years of famine. Believing him, the pharaoh ordered his charges to store up enough grain to last through the seven lean years.

Famine did indeed wrack the land, and the Israelites, having not been forewarned, traveled to Egypt to buy grain. Joseph's father and eleven brothers came to Egypt and were reunited with him. Seeing Joseph, now elevated to an important position as a reward for his prescience, the brothers recalled his prophecy that his father, mother, and brothers would honor him: "Behold, the sun, moon, and eleven stars were bowing down to me."

Like Joseph, the Old Testament prophet Daniel gained his freedom by interpreting the dreams of a king who had held him against his will. Describing the dream of Nebuchadnezzar, king of Babylon, Daniel said, "Thou sawest a great image whose brightness was terrible. The image's head was made of fine gold, his breast and his arms of silver, his belly and his thighs of brass. His legs of iron, his feet part of iron and part of clay. A stone, cut without hands, smote the image upon his feet. Then was the iron, the clay, the brass, the silver and the gold broken to pieces and became as chaff on the summer threshing floor." To the prophet, such symbolism was clear: The golden head represented Nebuchadnezzar as the ruler of a great dominion that encompassed virtually the entire world—which was the case. In the future, after Nebuchadnezzar's death, said Daniel, his huge empire would be succeeded by a series of less glorious kingdoms. The last of those kingdoms, represented by the dream statue's legs and feet, would be as strong as iron but also as brittle as the clay of which the feet were partly made and thus would collapse when struck with a rock. (Traditionally, biblical scholars have said Daniel was foretelling the Roman Empire and its fall a thousand years in the future—and he was incidentally bestowing eternal life on the phrase "feet of clay.") The king was so pleased with Daniel's explanation that he made the prophet his chief adviser.

The many gods of the early Greeks and Romans, like the one God of the Hebrews, used dreams to speak to humans. Zeus, father of the Greek gods, employed Hypnos, the god of sleep, and his son Morpheus, the god of dreams, to facilitate the transmission of messages to mortals. The winged messenger Hermes was usually charged with delivering such communications from on high as inspiration, advice, prophecies, and warnings.

Most Greeks thought of dreams as phantoms that

The Myth as Society's Dream

A lifelong student of the world's mythologies, Joseph Campbell (below) saw many links between myths and dreams. "A dream," he said, "is a personal experience of that deep, dark ground" underlying conscious life, while a myth is "society's dream. The myth is the public dream and the dream is the private myth," and both "are symbolic in the same general way of the dynamics of the psyche."

Although Campbell distinguished between personal dreams and archetypal, or mythic, dreams, he noted that many personal dreams have a mythic dimension. For example, a dreamer worrying about an upcoming test will dream of previous personal failures. The dream content, said Campbell, is "purely personal. But, on another level, the problem of passing an exam is not simply personal. Everyone has to pass a threshold of some kind. That is an archetypal thing." Thus a personal dream can have "a basic mythological theme." Images that symbolize "mysteries of universal import," noted Campbell, "are never experienced in a pure state," but they appear in many variations. He urged dreamers to try to see through "local features" to discern a dream's eternal themes.

Campbell called the realm that we enter in sleep "the infantile unconscious," the storehouse of "the basic images of ritual, mythology, and vision." Thus in history as well as in myths, he said, human life is enriched by the visions, ideas, and inspirations brought back from the dream world, from the "unquenched source through which society is reborn."

A Culture Shaped by Dreams

In the days when Native American cultures were in their glory, Indians cherished and depended on their dreams—as well as similar waking visions and trances—using them to shape every feature of tribal life. A Jesuit priest who was living among the Hurons in the seventeenth century observed: "The dream often presides in their councils; traffic, fishing, and hunting are undertaken usually under its sanction, and almost as if only to satisfy it. They hold nothing so precious that they would not readily deprive themselves of it for the sake of a dream. It prescribes their feasts, their dances, their songs, their games—in a word, the dream does everything and is in truth the principal God of the Hurons."

Not only the Hurons but all Native American tribes held dreams to be the source and foundation of spirituality. They believed that a dream was the soul's sojourn in another world, a realm independent of the dreamer. So real was this other world that, for instance, a Cherokee bitten by a snake in a dream would seek a healer's treatment for snakebite upon returning to the waking world.

Many dreams, of course, were considered ordinary and of no special account, but others were said to have power in them. In such a vision, the dreamer might see one of the tribe's gods or a revered animal. Through a dream a Native American might receive spiritual instructions about taking on a personal totem, choosing a life's work, or selecting garments and foods that would provide spiritual power. Some visions pertained to the life of the whole tribe, prescribing rituals and dances, songs and paint-

ings, cures and sacrifices, even the dispatching of war parties.

The two tribal artifacts pictured here were directly inspired by dreams. Below is the plan of a so-called sand painting, drawn on the ground with powdered pigments as part of the Navajo nine-day healing ceremony called the Night Way. Sacred pictures such as this one depicted Navajo gods and enlisted their help in restoring balance, health, and beauty to the life of an injured or unhappy member of the tribe. The tunic at right, painted with symbols that were revealed in a dream, was worn for the Arapaho Ghost Dance, a dream-inspired ritual widely celebrated by the hard-pressed tribes of the West in the latter part of the nineteenth century.

If the symbols involved in such dream-given objects look cryptic and perhaps awkward to outside eyes, it is because they were meant not as art or decoration but as holy things, reminders of a deep spiritual experience. An example is a dream-inspired Teton Sioux song that said simply, "owls/ hooting/ in the passing of the night/ owls hooting." Speaking of such a song's rich but concealed meanings, a Native American woman remarked, "The song is very short because we know so much."

Dreams with power in them were greatly desired. They not only brought new spiritual gifts for the tribe, they conferred great prestige upon the dreamers. And although such visions sometimes came unbidden in sleep, the majority of the tribes developed sacred practices in an effort to increase the likelihood of having dreams with power in them.

The vision quest, a ritual to induce spiritually potent dreams, was a common part of the rites that marked an Indian's passage from childhood into adulthood. A vision quest typically included fasting, isolation, sleeplessness, perhaps even self-inflicted physical pain. In order to prepare the child for the impending ordeal, counseling from parents or a shaman sometimes began when he or she was just six or seven years old.

Originally inspired by a vision, this traditional Navajo drawing invoked the healing power of a tribal deity, the Black God, symbolized by the cornstalk. The people all face the god in reverence.

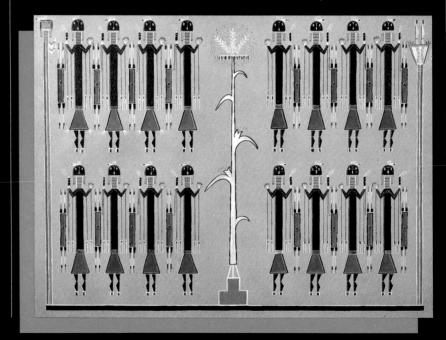

Many Indian tribes taught daughters as well as sons to seek the gods' favor through visions; in some tribes, the girls could drop the quest at puberty, when they gained the power to bear children. Many tribes believed that a successful vision quest was absolutely essential if one was to attain a successful life; among the members of the Crow tribe, anyone whose vision quest failed was permitted to buy a part—a song, perhaps—of someone else's vision-gained spiritual power.

To invite visions at a later stage of life, many tribes relied on dream incubation, the practice of sleeping in a place of special spiritual power. The Plains tribes, such as the Crow, Blackfoot, and Cheyenne, believed that the most powerful sacred site was the top of a prominent mountain.

As white settlement spread and Native American tribes were confined to reservations, many warriors were left with dreams that they could not put to use. A Chippewa man might dream a song to be sung in battle, to help him face death—but going to war was forbidden by the laws of the white man. The dreamer would then make a banner bearing an emblem of his powerful dream and would fasten it to a pole in front of his house. His neighbors would know that he was burdened with a song he would never be able to sing—but he also was believed to possess the power to heal and the ability to face death.

A turtle and a crescent moon, symbolic of the material world, are engulfed by birds and stars representing spiritual life, on this dream-inspired Arapaho dress.

were capable of assuming different forms in their visits to sleeping mortals. Thus the Greeks never said they "had" dreams, rather they "saw" them, and these phantoms were said to "visit" and "stand over" a dreamer. Phantoms could take the shape of gods, ghosts, or the image of someone known to the dreamer. In Homer's *Iliad,* the ghost of Patroklos, Achilles' dearest friend, pays the sleeping warrior a visit. "And there appeared to him the ghost of unhappy Patroklos all in his likeness for stature, and the lovely eyes, and voice, and wore such clothing as Patroklos had worn on his body. The ghost came and stood over his head and spoke a word to him," which was to say that Achilles had dreamed his dead friend's visit.

Elsewhere in the *Iliad,* Homer noted that the Greek gods did not hesitate to use false dreams as a means of punishing wrongdoers. He wrote that the war god Zeus sent such a dream-message to King Agamemnon in the shape of a trusted counselor, because Agamemnon had stolen a servant girl from the warrior Achilles. Zeus commanded, "Go forth, evil dream, . . . to . . . Agamemnon; speak to him in words exactly as I command you." The phantom Nestor tells Agamemnon it is time to assemble his army and attack the city of Troy, for the gods are on his side and victory is assured. Buoyed by false hopes, believing his fate to be in the hands of benevolent gods, Agamemnon decided to attack—and lost.

As King Agamemnon's disastrous decision proved, it was not always easy to distinguish between a true dream and a false one. Given the ambiguity of some dreams, it is not surprising that the Greeks, like the peoples of earlier cultures, turned to soothsayers or interpreters in order to understand the significance of their dreams.

They also evolved rituals to induce dreams they believed to be healing. The sick traveled to temples, especially to the most famous temple of Aesculapius—the god of medicine—at Epidaurus, in the hope that the deity would visit them in sleep.

Such induction of dreams, practiced throughout the Middle East, depended on careful preparation. The faithful were expected to abstain from sex and certain foods, such as broad beans, that were believed to inhibit dreams, and they even underwent a ritual cold-water cleansing. They were then permitted to enter the temple. After making offerings to the gods and attending lengthy sermons and prayer services, the seekers went to sleep atop the skins of sacrificed animals, in a room filled with the writhing, but harmless, yellow snakes that were the symbol of Aesculapius.

In this classical Greek temple sculpture, a man is healed by incubation, the dream-cure. In his dream his spirit leaves his body (right) to receive the god's help (left), while healing power, symbolized by a snake, ministers to the body's ailing shoulder.

Instant cures were often reported. But more commonly, patients woke to report that Aesculapius had indeed visited them in a dream and recommended herbal remedies or a change in diet. Aristedes, a second-century Greek writer who suffered from toothaches, earaches, asthma, and cramps, among other ailments, dreamed that Aesculapius advised him to take cold baths, walk barefoot, and ride horseback. Following the god's advice, he tore off his clothes in front of a group of startled onlookers and jumped into a freezing river. His illnesses allegedly disappeared.

Universal Symbols: The Snake

Dreams are often couched in the language of symbols, using images of familiar things to point to another level of reality. Symbols are found in the dreams, myths, religion, and art of all cultures, at every stage of technological development. And while some figures serve as symbols in only one culture, others are universal, charged with transcendent meaning by peoples everywhere. On this and the next two pages are three such symbols: the snake, fire, and water.

The snake—or serpent or dragon—is one of the oldest symbols, found with fertility goddesses in some of the world's earliest sculptures. As a symbol, the serpent embodies dual qualities, derived from the living animal. Because it lives in the ground, the snake is an emblem of the nurturing earth but also of the unknown dangers of the underworld. Christian imagery emphasizes the dark side, casting the serpent, the evil tempter in the Garden of Eden, as a spiritual threat; but many early American peoples worshiped serpent gods, and some Indian yogis revere the serpent as a spiritual guide.

Many ancients, including the Greeks, attributed healing power to the snake *(above)*, a belief preserved in the caduceus, the snake-entwined staff symbolizing the medical profession. In psychoanalytic terms, a snake, with its dual above- and underground nature, can signal a merging of conscious and unconscious, leading to new growth and maturity.

Another believer, Clinates of Thebes, was infested with lice. Clinates visited Epidaurus and dreamed that the god had undressed him and swept away the vermin with a broom; in the morning the lice had vanished. Numerous other patients inscribed the walls of the temple with similar testimony to their cures. But whether divine dreams alone can be credited with such healing is open to question; some sources say that temple priests often whispered messages to sleepers through holes bored in the walls above their heads.

Dream healing continued unabated even as medicine was emerging as a fledgling science in Greece, and the two existed side by side. Those who were ill consulted physicians but continued to seek counsel in their dreams, often calling on the medical practitioners to help administer dream-dictated treatments. An appreciative view of the value of dreams in regard to health is found in the written works of Hippocrates, the father of medicine. Yet the great physician, who is thought to have written the first Western medical dream book, *Treatise on Dreams,* around the fourth century BC, did not adhere to the belief that all dreams were sent by gods. "Some dreams are divinely inspired," he wrote, "but others are the direct result of the physical body."

Hippocrates believed, as do many physicians today, that a direct link existed between the mind and the body and that dreams provided a clue to one's physical condition. For example, the treatise states that dreaming of the color black symbolizes sickness, whereas dreaming of flight symbolizes mental derangement. Hippocrates also claimed that dreams could foretell disease. "If the heavenly bodies are seen dimly in a clear sky, and shine weakly and seem to be stopped from revolving by dryness, then it is a sign that there is a danger of incurring sickness. Exercise should be stopped," the Greek physician recommended. A star's upward movement, he continued, "indicates fluxes in the head," while movement into the sea signaled disease of the bowels, and "eastward movement, the growing of tumors in the flesh."

Fire: Friend and Foe

Fire stands with earth, air, and water as one of the four ancient elements, the building blocks of existence. Its primal presence and paradoxical nature make it a compelling if ambiguous symbol in dreams everywhere. Fire generates heat and light while destroying its fuel; it fascinates with endless lively movement yet is constant; it can sustain life or end it; it can destroy matter or transform and purify it. Fire represents friend and enemy, comfort and danger, divinity and damnation. Its continual energy makes fire a potent symbol of life, even eternal life, but also portends eternal torment in hell. When it is cozily banked on the hearth or in the industrial furnace, fire is a wild thing temporarily trapped in a cage of human devising.

In dreams, fire can mean transformation, purification, spiritual illumination, love, passion, and sexuality; much depends on the context. A small, tame fire may signify peace and contentment, while fire uncontrolled is a primary symbol of destruction. Fire consuming a house could indicate harm or death to a person, perhaps someone ill and "burning up" with a fever. Fire as represented by the sun would probably mean agreeable warmth and nurturance for a dreamer in a temperate climate, but for one near the Equator, the sun would represent a dangerous, perhaps life-threatening power. A large fire can simply represent some powerful force over which the dreamer lacks conscious control.

In many mythic traditions, a hero steals fire from the gods. Although this is a life-transforming feat, it is also one that entails some regret and guilt about challenging the rule of respected deities—or, in psychological truth, parents. In dream interpretation, obtaining fire may signify attaining a new level of understanding or maturity and leaving the old behind, encompassing all the elation, fear, and guilt attendant on such a passage.

Some of the Greeks, anticipating modern approaches, abandoned the idea of outside agents altogether. One of those was the fourth-century philosopher Plato, who suggested that if all aspects of a person's life were in balance, an individual would find true awareness in dreams, and submitted that dreams can often boil up from a human being's primitive cauldron of emotions. "In all of us, even in good men, there is a lawless wild-beast nature which peers out in sleep."

Neither did Plato's younger contemporary Aristotle believe that dreams were divinely inspired. In his essays *On Sleep and Waking, On Dreams,* and *On Prophecy in Sleep,* Aristotle argued that if the gods sent dreams, they would send them only to intelligent and rational people. Since dreams are not restricted to the learned, wrote Aristotle, they could not be messages from the gods. He said that dreams that were thought to be prophetic were actually the result of coincidence or unconscious suggestion. In *On Dreams,* he explained, "When we are about to act, or are engaged in any course of action, or have already performed certain actions, we often find ourselves concerned with these actions, or performing them in a vivid dream; the cause whereof is that the dream-movement has had a way paved for it from the original movement set up in the daytime."

Yet Aristotle recognized the importance of dreams. In his treatise *On Divination,* the philosopher records that physicians "tell us that one should pay diligent attention to dreams, and to hold this view is reasonable also for those who are not physicians but speculative philosophers." He even conceded that some dreams might provide a clue to health problems. He felt that the mind is better able to focus on small internal factors when asleep than awake, stating, "It is obvious that the beginnings of sickness and the other accidents that are produced in the body . . . are necessarily clearer in sleep than in the waking state." During sleep, Aristotle pointed out, the mind might suggest a course of treatment within a dream.

But Plato and Aristotle were unusual for their—or any—age. Most Greeks had no doubt that dreams were sent by the gods and were only concerned with discovering the hidden meanings of the mysterious messages. They flocked to dream interpreters, one of the most famous being the soothsayer Artemidorus Daldianus, who lived in the second century AD. Artemidorus recorded more than 3,000 dreams in a five-volume treatise titled *Oneirocritica* (The Interpretation of Dreams). And if dreams can be said to mirror reality, life in the Greco-Roman world of his era was anything but tame. Throughout the pages of *Oneirocritica* appear accounts of especially disquieting, even brutal, dreams—a man sacrifices his wife and sells her remains to the local butcher; another skins his son alive; still another eats his own excrement.

Artemidorus classified and interpreted these dreams, identifying five different types—symbolic and prophetic dreams, fantasies, nightmares, and daytime visions. Unlike most of his contemporaries, he stressed that dream symbols and images must be analyzed in the context of the dream and, more important, that the dream must be interpreted in relation to the individual dreamer. These beliefs contradicted other soothsayers, who ascribed fixed meanings to symbols—that dreaming of a snake, for example, foretold illness—without regard to the dreamer's circumstances. Artemidorus noted that symbols could mean one thing to one dreamer and the opposite to another.

Yet Artemidorus did identify some symbols to set up a framework for dream interpretation. Many have compared his approach with that of modern psychoanalysts. Like Freud, the Greek dream consultant ascribed sexual connotations to certain symbols. He claimed that sowing, seeding, and tilling, for example, referred to the desire to marry and have children. He ascribed a phallic symbolism to the plow and wrote that horses, carriages, and ditches dug in the soil represented a wife or concubine.

No record exists to vouch for Artemidorus's popularity

Water: Source of Life

Cradle and origin of all forms of living beings, water is everywhere that life is. Like fire, water has a dual nature. It is womb and grave, sustainer and destroyer, purifier and spoiler. Flowing in a river or ocean, water embodies constant change and movement but also has permanence. Though paired with fire as an essential for life, water offers a heavier, slower, more comforting presence. Since it purifies without destroying, water figures in the rites of many religions. The water of baptism especially suggests the waters of birth and symbolizes the start of a new life.

Although water epitomizes passivity and yieldingness, the traditional feminine principle, it should not be mistaken for powerlessness. In Taoist thought, water embodies the power of weakness, adaptability, and fluidity: Even as the water in a stream parts to flow around a rock, it wears the rock away.

In dreams, still water may suggest the womb, prenatal security, and bliss; crashing waves may represent external power beyond the dreamer's control or his or her own sexual urges. A swimming pool may symbolize leisure or competition. When it appears as an expanse concealing mysteries, water is a symbol for the unconscious. Water's dual nature makes the comparison apt: Chaotic and potentially violent, the unconscious is also the sustaining source of conscious life. Diving into water can symbolize a search for life's meaning, and crossing over water may signify a transformation, a passage from one condition to another.

A Priest Who Dreamed the Future

Many biblical figures received messages from God while asleep, but reports of such revealing dreams are not confined to the Bible. In one modern case, a devout nine-year-old by the name of Giovanni Bosco had a dream in 1825 he later called prophetic.

He dreamed he punched a gang of tough boys in his Italian village to stop their cursing. A luminous man 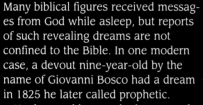 appeared and told him he must win boys over with kindness, not violence. "Who are you?" Giovanni asked. Replied the image: "I am the son of her whom your mother taught you to salute three times a day." Then a woman in a sparkling cloak showed him some wild animals that became lambs as he watched. "What you see happening to these an- imals," she said, "you must make happen for my children."

Giovanni became a priest and founded a home for boys and the Salesian Order, made up of monks who care for homeless children. Father Bosco had many visionary dreams: He sometimes knew a boy's sins before hearing the child's confession, and he foresaw the deaths of several boys. Bosco died in 1888, and in 1934, he was declared a saint.

Father Bosco (right) confesses one of his resident boys in the open, an arrangement that he preferred to the closed confessional.

in his day. But most dream books published thereafter drew upon his exhaustive research and observations, and when *Oneirocritica* was finally translated into English 1500 years after his death, it went through two dozen printings in less than a century.

Although throughout the ages people have continued to disagree about just what any particular dream signifies—and even what dreams are and where they come from—there is wide agreement that some dreams have changed the course of history. Dream scholar Raymond de Becker has described dreams as "the revealer of an energy at work in the depths of individuals and peoples. This energy often directs men without their knowledge and is found at the roots of the greatest catastrophes and the most sublime creations."

The energy of dreams has inspired soldiers, scientists, poets, and politicians, who in turn have influenced the lives of millions. Otto von Bismarck, the militaristic German chancellor, claimed that a prophetic dream convinced him to continue his 1866 campaign against the Austrians. German pharmacologist Otto Loewi allegedly credited a 1920 dream with revealing an experiment that helped prove his theory on the chemical transmission of nerve impulses—and win him the 1936 Nobel Prize for medicine. And legend has it that Joan of Arc based her life on visions that came to her regularly in dreams and in waking hours. In George Bernard Shaw's play *St. Joan,* a critic scorns her dreams as figments of her imagination. "Of course," she replies, "that is how messages of God do come."

Indeed, by tradition, the origins of many of the world's religions, including Christianity, Buddhism, and Islam, are intertwined with accounts of divinely inspired dreams. The Old Testament tells of God revealing himself to Abraham and Jacob in dreams, and it is through a dream that the Hebrew warrior Gideon is assured of a victory over the desert-dwelling Midianites. In the New Testament, the apostle Matthew relates four heavenly messages sent to Joseph, the husband of Jesus' mother, Mary, through his dreams. In the first, Joseph is contemplating the disturbing pregnancy of his then betrothed, Mary, whom he believed to be a virgin. "Then Joseph . . . was minded to put her away, . . . but while he thought on these things, behold the angel of the Lord appeared unto him in a dream, saying, Joseph, thou son of David, fear not to take unto thee Mary thy wife: for that which is conceived in her is of the Holy Ghost. And she shall bring forth a son, and thou shall call his name Jesus: for he shall save his people from their sins. . . . Then Joseph being raised from sleep as the angel of the Lord had bidded him, and took unto him his wife."

When an angel next invaded his dreams and warned him to flee to Egypt to save Mary's newborn son from King Herod, Joseph again obeyed, and he remained in Egypt until he was told of Herod's death in a third dream: "Arise and take the young child and his mother and go into the land of Israel: for they are dead which sought the young child's life." Finally, in a fourth episode, "being warned of God in a dream, he turned aside into the parts of Galilee" and then settled there.

In each of these cases, Joseph did not hesitate to follow the advice in his dreams. Matthew also tells us that the three wise men were "warned of God in a dream that they should not return to Herod," in order to save the life of the infant Jesus. To a believer, these dreams were unquestionably messages from God.

All of the biblical dreams were presented as supernatural revelations, and their meanings were startlingly clear. But the full import hidden by the rich symbolism of the dreams that surrounded the birth and life of Buddha, or "the Enlightened One," was not always immediately perceptible to the dreamers. The woman who would become Buddha's mother, Maya, experienced one such dream, which she presented to practiced dream interpreters for their opinion. "White as snow or silver, more brilliant than the moon or the sun," she described, "the best of elephants, with fine feet, well-balanced, with strong joints, with six tusks hard as adamant, the magnanimous, the very beauti-

Dreams and Films: From the Same Factory

Movies, with their near-magical manipulations of images, seem to be tailor-made to express dreams. Naturally enough, some of the most eminent filmmakers have turned their dreams to artistic advantage.

Italian director Federico Fellini has called dreams "fables we tell ourselves, myths that help us understand." In his films, he said, he strives to create "a stimulating ambiguity between fantasy and reality." In movies such as his classic *8½*, Fellini is at times resolutely obscure about where reality ends and the dream begins. And many of his characters are so physically grotesque and his settings so disturbingly surreal that one can only suppose they were dream inspired. Moreover, he has said he employs color on the screen not only as part of the language of cinema but to convey "the idea and the feeling of the dream."

Swedish movie giant Ingmar Bergman goes even further than Fellini in relating his films to dreams. "All my

pictures are dreams," Bergman has said. And indeed, some of his cinematic images are outright presentations of characters' dreams. Two of his films —*Wild Strawberries* and *The Naked Night*—contain scenes that Bergman calls faithful copies of his own dreams. But even when the content is not drawn directly from his sleeping visions, his films have many dreamlike qualities. Among the most famous is the Dance of Death *(bottom)*, a powerful sequence from *The Seventh Seal.* In the same film, Death *(below)*, played by Bengt Ekerot, maintains an iconic, dreamlike presence.

Bergman's work, however, shares more than images with dreams. For him, making films—like dreaming—is one of life's essentials. Scientists studying sleep, he noted, "discovered that if you are prevented from dreaming you go crazy. It is the same with me. If I could not create my dreams—my films—that would make me completely crazy. Dreams are a sort of creative process, don't you think? My films come from the same factory."

Bergman notes that like dreams, film "escapes the control of the intellect almost voluptuously." In film, he says, "we go straight to the feelings. Only afterwards we can start to work with our intellect."

Bergman has used the same actors again and again in his movies so that their faces have become hauntingly familiar, much like the archetypal figures that appear in dreams. His many films, taken together, form what one critic has described as "a tapestry of recurring dreams." Bergman welcomes such comparisons, saying that if audiences find his dreams "close to their dreams, I think that is the best communication."

ful has entered my womb." The interpreters, foretelling the birth of the chosen one, predicted, "A son will be born to Maya. Issue of a royal line, the magnanimous one will be a universal monarch; . . . he will become a wandering monk; . . . by the sweetness of his ambrosia, he will be able to satisfy all worlds."

Some years later, Buddha's father, King Cudhodana, dreamed he saw his son leave the house escorted by a troop of gods "and then set forth, a wandering monk, clad in a reddish garment." When the king awoke, he asked servants whether the young prince was still at home. He was, but the king was not consoled. "Of course he will leave, my young prince," the sovereign lamented, "since these portents have appeared to me."

Buddha's leaving did not occur until many years later, after he had married and become a father himself. In fact, the most fantastic dream recorded in Buddhist writings was actually a series of dreams experienced one night by Gopa, Buddha's wife. In these visions she saw herself completely naked, with both hands and feet cut off; she saw the earth quaking, the ocean raised, and the axis of the world shaken to its foundations; she witnessed a meteor leaving the town and the city plunged into darkness, her husband's possessions broken and scattered. Awakened, terrified by her nightmare, Gopa asked Buddha what it meant. He replied, "Be of good cheer, you have not seen anything evil" and explained the meaning of each of the disasters she recount-

ed—all stemming from her anguish over her husband's imminent departure from home and family to embrace the life of a wandering monk. That she experienced such pain in her dream, said Buddha, was a sign that she was capable of attaining perfection.

In the case of Islam, dreams are thought by some to have provided the actual building blocks of the religion. According to Islamic teachings, the first surah, or chapter, of the Koran, the religion's sacred scripture, was delivered to Muhammad by the angel Gabriel as the Prophet slept. And in the Hadith, a companion piece to the Koran that guides followers of Islam in daily life, the Prophet is described as receiving subsequent surahs while lying in a trance or dreamlike state, sweating and shivering and with his eyes closed. It is said that Muhammad was so strong a believer in the importance of dreams that each morning after awakening he would explain his dreams to his disciples and then interpret theirs. Indeed, after one of his disciples dreamed of a calling to prayer, Muhammad instituted the *adhan*, in which a muezzin summons the faithful to prayer from the minaret of a mosque.

It seems that many great events throughout the ages, religious and secular, were preceded by relevant human dreams. Tradition offers stories of dreams that allegedly inspired great political leaders, predicted the outcomes of battles or wars, and determined the course of historical developments by alerting key figures to circumstances that, if not

Tippu Sahib, an Indian warrior-sultan of the eighteenth century, made records of his dreams and based his battle tactics on some of those visions.

foreseen, could have cost them their lives or their ambitions. For instance, the Greek historian Herodotus records that Xerxes, a fifth-century-BC Persian emperor, was deeply troubled by a dream in which a figure of a man appeared and warned the inexperienced ruler not to cancel an impending attack on Greece, as his military advisers had recently recommended. Disregarding the nocturnal advice, Xerxes agreed to call off preparations for the massive invasion. The next night he was again visited in his dream by the spirit, who said, "So you have openly, in the presence of your subjects, renounced the campaign and made light of what I said to you, as if it had never been said at all. Now let me tell you what the result will be, if you do not at once undertake this war: just as in a moment you rose to greatness and power, so in a moment you will be brought low again."

Terrified, Xerxes leaped from his bed and summoned his uncle and chief advisor, Artabanus. The elder tried to soothe the young king, explaining that the dream was not a divine prophecy but merely contained "the shadows of what we have been thinking about during the day." Xerxes was unconvinced. As a compromise, Artabanus agreed to wear the king's nightclothes and sleep in his bed to see whether the dream would come again.

That night the dream phantom confronted Artabanus. "Are you the man who in would-be concern for the King is trying to dissuade him from making war on Greece? You will not escape unpunished, either now or hereafter, for seeking to turn aside the course of destiny." Just as the phantom was about to burn out the adviser's eyes with hot irons, Artabanus awakened. He ran to Xerxes and said to him, "Now I know that God is at work in this matter; and since apparently Heaven itself is about to send ruin upon Greece, I admit that I was mistaken. . . . Prepare for war . . . and as God is offering you this great opportunity, play your own part to the full in realizing it."

Xerxes amassed an incredible force of fighting men and marched into Greece. The war he launched—and supposedly would have averted, had it not been for his dream—raged for two years, finally concluding in 479 BC with defeats that sent the Persian forces home and put an end once and for all to their ambitions of conquering Greece. If the Persian deity really did come to Xerxes in a dream, his divine advice on the war was obviously faulty. Neither, apparently, did the god forewarn Xerxes of his death—he was murdered by conspirators.

It seems Xerxes was not the only warrior to be misled by his dreams. According to Roman historian Valerius Maximus, the Carthaginian general Hannibal dreamed about invading Rome before he did so in real life. He saw "a young man, as beautiful as an angel," who said he had been sent from heaven to urge Hannibal to invade Italy. When Hannibal saw an immense serpent destroying everything in its path, he asked the young man what it meant. "You see the ruin of Italy and the disasters which await it," replied the young man. "Go! The fates are going to be accomplished." In 219 BC, the Carthaginian led 40,000 men and a parade of elephants across the Alps to march on Rome.

Valerius Maximus adds, "Is there any need to recall the evils with which Hannibal ravaged Italy after he had this dream and obeyed its instructions?" Perhaps not, but it should be remembered that, in spite of his prophetic vision, Hannibal failed to crush Rome. When the Romans finally demanded his surrender, the general committed suicide by taking poison.

When a Dictator Seized a Nation's Sleep

In every waking moment, warned a Nazi official, every German must be "a soldier of Adolf Hitler"; the only remaining "private matter," he insisted, was sleep. But not even sleep was a refuge from Hitler *(at right, below)* and his dictatorship.

Just after the Nazi takeover in 1933, Charlotte Beradt, a young journalist in Germany, began asking acquaintances to tell her their dreams—and discovered a living example of a people's collective unconscious being shaped by a common mass experience. She recorded hundreds of dreams in coded notes that she hid in book bindings or sent to friends abroad. Despite her precautions, however, many people were afraid to relate their dreams, fearful of what they might reveal. Several reported the identical vision: "I dreamt that it was forbidden to dream but I did anyway."

Unlike soldiers in combat, who suffer violent dreams of gory dismemberment, civilians at home under this totalitarian rule endured visions of psychological coercion, the bloodless destruction of dignity and identity. One such dreamer was a manufacturer who, in order to keep his factory, pretended allegiance to the Reich he actually hated. The man dreamed that Propaganda Minister Goebbels visited the factory and commanded him to give a stiff-armed Nazi salute, in front of all the workers. The manufacturer found he was unable to lift his arm. He kept trying, and after half an hour of agonized effort, finally succeeded—whereupon Goebbels, who had watched the struggle impassively, said, "I don't want your salute," and walked away, leaving the factory owner frozen in humiliation.

Some dreamers distilled the Third Reich's domestic terror tactics into surreal images. One man dreamed that he was enjoying an evening at home reading a book, when he looked up to find that the walls of his apartment, and every wall as far as he could see, had suddenly disappeared. Another man related his dream about unreal but plausible surveillance agencies—the Monitoring Office and the Training Center for the Wall-Installation of Listening Devices.

Many people, caught between pressure from the Reich and the dictates of conscience, relived in their dreams the intolerable choices forced upon them. One young woman, who was prompted by the anti-Semitic racial laws to end her engagement to a Jewish man, dreamed that she tried to argue with Hitler's criticism of her fiancé but was advised by a friend, "There's not a thing one can do."

One who fared better in following his dreams was Alexander the Great, the Macedonian conqueror of most of the known world. Alexander strongly believed in the prophetic power of dreams and retained a personal interpreter to assist with dream divination. Once, while his forces were attacking the city of Tyros, on the coast of Lebanon, in the summer of 332 BC, Alexander dreamed that a satyros—a nature spirit—had danced on his shield. Aristander, his interpreter, explained that the dream contained a visual pun and that by rearranging the letters in the Greek letters of the word *satyros* he could spell out the message, "Tyros is thine." Guided by this divination, Alexander renewed his attack on the city and was victorious.

Three centuries later, the military plans of another famous warrior were confirmed in a dream. The night before Julius Caesar led his army across the Rubicon to march against his own beloved Rome, he dreamed that he slept with his mother. Apparently Caesar saw this as a signal that the invasion should go forward, for he proceeded to attack the city and, to his relief, encountered little resistance. Ironically, the Roman general and statesman later failed to heed another dream—that of his wife, Calpurnia, who warned him to "beware the Ides of March." Disregarding that prophetic message cost him his life.

Even so eminent a military strategist as Napoleon Bonaparte was said to use his dreams to plan his campaigns. When he awoke, Napoleon would jot down the details of all his nightly visions. Later, the French general

Two great nineteenth-century authors whose work by some accounts was inspired by dreams voiced diametrically opposite responses to such suggestions. Robert Louis Stevenson (above), a Scot with strong beliefs in Little People, credited his "Brownies, God bless them" with delivering "printable and profitable tales" to him in dreams. But practical Englishman Charles Dickens, although an artist of his own era portrayed him (right) dozing in his study amid dreamlike visions of his characters, denied ever dreaming of his creations and doubted that any author could. "It would be," he stated, "like a man's dreaming of meeting himself, which is clearly an impossibility."

would test the strategies by positioning toy soldiers in a sandbox. Before he confronted his enemies on the field at Waterloo, Napoleon supposedly had a dream about a black cat that ran between opposing armies, and he saw his own forces decimated. If this is true, he must have chosen to ignore the dream's warning; his defeat at Waterloo sealed the fate of his empire.

For all that these visions foreshadowed—the victories, defeats, death and destruction—perhaps none were as dra-

matic or held such portent for the future as the dream that a young German soldier claimed to have experienced at Somme on a November night in 1917, during World War I. According to the story, the sky was moonless and the frigid, dank air was still. There was a lull in the usual deadly artillery bombardment, and a group of German infantrymen slept soundly within their earthen cocoon, a small dugout fetid with the acrid smell of gunpowder, rotting food, and unwashed clothes.

But one German, a twenty-eight-year-old corporal, was having trouble sleeping. A terrifying nightmare played across his mind as he tossed and turned in his bunk. He dreamed that he was being buried alive beneath tons of earth and molten iron. Warm blood flowed across his chest. He was choking.

Suddenly he awakened, realizing that he had been dreaming but worried nevertheless. "Is it a forewarning?" he began to ask himself. All was quiet outside. The corporal rose from his bed and left the cramped bunker. The night air was crisp. He stepped over the rampart of the trench and began to walk—as if he was still in the throes of a dream—into the no man's land that separated the German lines from the French. Unarmed, he suddenly perceived that he was in grave danger.

A screaming burst of gunfire quickly brought the soldier to his senses. A heavy artillery shell exploded nearby with a deafening roar. The rifle fire ceased. The young infantryman turned and scrambled back toward the safety of the bunker. But a French shell had scored a direct hit, cav-

Cosima Wagner, seen here with husband Richard, faithfully recorded in her own diary the composer's descriptions of almost 300 of his dreams. Most were sagas of personal rejection and botched concerts.

ing in the earthen nest where a few minutes earlier he had been sleeping. His fellow soldiers lay entombed under tons of dirt and rubble. Only the lone corporal, who would later be known to the world as Adolf Hitler, survived to tell of the terror of that night and of the premonitory dream that had saved his life.

Whether or not any credence at all can be placed in tales of the prophetic power of dreams, there does seem to be a wealth of anecdotal evidence that dreams can indeed be a force in creative inspiration. The collected testimonies of scientists, philosophers, writers, and musicians make a strong case for the positive impact of visions that have graced their sleep.

The seventeenth-century French mathematician René Descartes, hailed as the father of modern philosophy, held that dreams were not functions of the rational mind; they were merely fantasies or unfulfilled wishes. Nonetheless, Descartes credited a series of dreams he had as a young man with inspiring his life's work.

The then twenty-three-year-old mathematician was spending the winter of 1619 in Germany, and on the evening of November 10, he had just returned from the emperor's coronation at Frankfurt. During the night's slumber he experienced three dreams, which he later said could only have come from above. The first two of these visions were filled with terrifying phantoms, violent winds, thunder, and flashing sparks. The third dream, in which he discovered and read a dictionary as well as an anthology of poetry, was ultimately the most memorable. Indeed, Descartes was so moved by this final dream that, according to one biographer, "he not only decided while sleeping that it was a dream, but also interpreted it before sleep left him."

To Descartes the dream was a revelation. He suddenly realized that science (symbolized by the dictionary) and philosophy (symbolized by the anthology of poetry) should be linked. Why not apply the disciplines of science, with its requirement of observational or experimental proof of any hypothesis, to philosophical matters? The young Frenchman was so shaken by his dreams that he needed a few days to recover. When he next took pen to paper, however, the words and thoughts flowed with ease. He devoted the rest of his life to formulating a philosophy that would forever change the way Western intellectuals think. Yet that same work, by characterizing a sleeper's dreams as nothing more than fanciful images or unsatisfied desires, denounced the very source of its inspiration. As one writer noted, Descartes's was "the dream that would eventually put an end to dreaming."

More than two centuries later, in 1869, Russian chemist Dmitry Mendeleyev would also credit his dreams with providing the key to a scientific puzzle. A professor of chemistry at the technological institute at St. Petersburg, Mendeleyev had for years been searching for a way not only to classify the chemical elements according to their atomic weights but to develop a system with which he could predict the discovery of then unknown elements. One night, after a long and fruitless day at work on the problem, he fell into an exhausted sleep. In his dreams appeared "a table where all the elements fell into place as required." On waking, he carefully recorded what would become the now universally familiar periodic table of the elements. Mendeleyev subsequently noted that "only in one place did a correction later seem necessary." Using this, he was able two years later to predict the existence of three new elements and assign them properties; within fifteen years, those elements were discovered.

Nineteenth-century inventor Elias Howe said his greatest invention was made possible by a similar dream experience. For years he had been working to develop a lock-stitch sewing machine. Progress had come to a halt, however, because Howe's needle design, which had a hole in the middle of the shank, did not work. His frustration at his inability to design a suitable needle had apparently reached its peak. One night in 1844 Howe dreamed of being captured by a tribe of savages. Their king roared, "Elias Howe, I command you on pain of death to finish this machine at once." But in his dream, as in conscious thought, the proper needle design eluded him. The tribal lord then ordered his warriors to execute Howe. Through his fear and panic, with the clarity sometimes afforded in a dream, the inventor noticed that at the business end of each warrior's spear was an eye-shaped hole. When he awoke, Howe bounded from bed to whittle a model of the needle he had

When eighteenth-century violinist Giuseppi Tartini found himself "enchanted" by music that the devil played for him in a dream, he immediately awoke and rushed to capture what he could remember. Although the resulting sonata, called the Devil's Trill, became his most celebrated work, one account says the composer found it so "far below" what he heard in his dream that he would have given up music if he could have found another livelihood.

seen in his dream—one with an eye-shaped hole near the point. It worked.

Dreams have also been the driving force behind many a literary achievement. In 1798, Samuel Taylor Coleridge, who was then treating an ailment with an opium-based drug, dozed off while he was reading in his Somerset, England, farmhouse. He later wrote that during this three-hour nap he composed not fewer than 200 to 300 lines of poetry. When he awoke, Coleridge began to write, his mind spewing forth word for word the lines of poetry that had come to him in his dream. He had transcribed only 54 lines of the poem when he was interrupted by a knock on the door. When he returned to his work after answering the door, he could remember no more of the eerily beautiful poetic fragment "Kubla Khan."

Robert Louis Stevenson maintained that complete stories regularly came to him in dreams. In an essay called "Chapter on Dreams," he said that he owed his inspiration to what he called the Little People or Brownies who populated his sleeping visions. "In time of need he sets to belaboring his brains after a story," the author wrote of himself, "and behold! At once the Little People bestir themselves in the same quest and all night long set before him the truncheons of tales upon their lighted theater."

Stevenson claimed that he never knew how his dreams—or his stories—would end. He noted that once he had no idea of a leading character's motive until she explained herself in the dream's final scene. "They [the Little People] can tell him a story, piece by piece, like a serial to keep him all the while in ignorance of where they aim," wrote Stevenson. The Brownies, he said, "do half my work for me while I am fast asleep, and in all human likelihood, do the rest for me as well when I am awake and fondly suppose I do it for myself."

On one occasion, however, a story did not come so readily to Stevenson. He had long been attempting to compose a tale about a man who led a double life, but the storyteller's well had seemingly run dry. Then, as the writer later related, "I dreamed a scene at the window, and the scene afterwards split in two, in which Hyde, pursued for some crime, took the powder and underwent the change in the presence of his pursuers." When he awoke, Stevenson was able to sit down to write what would subsequently become the classic horror story of good and evil, *The Strange Case of Dr. Jekyll and Mr. Hyde.*

Many other artists, including musicians such as Mozart and Schumann, claim to have first heard their compositions in their dreams. For Richard Wagner, musical ideas sometimes took shape during what he called trances, which some psychologists interpret as the hypnagogic state, the borderline period between waking and sleeping. During one such episode, he experienced a hallucination that he described in his autobiography, *My Life,* begun in 1865. "I sank into a kind of somnambulistic state, in which I suddenly had the feeling of being immersed in rapidly flowing water. Its rushing soon resolved itself for me into the musical sound of the chord of E flat major, resounding in persistent broken chords; these in turn transformed themselves into melodic figurations of increasing motion, yet the E flat major triad never changed, and seemed by its continuance to impart infinite significance to the element in which I was sinking." What Wagner heard in his hallucination would become a principal motif of his monumental operatic cycle, *The Ring of the Nibelung.*

But only one composer, it seems, boasted of making a pact with the devil in his dreams. Giuseppe Tartini, an eighteenth-century Italian composer, once dreamed that the devil agreed to become his servant if the musician would help him escape from a bottle. Once the devil had gained his freedom, Tartini gave him his violin to see if he could play it. "What was my astonishment when I heard him play with consummate skill a sonata of such exquisite beauty that it surpasses the most audacious dreams of my imagination. I was delighted, transported, enchanted," said Tartini. The composer awoke and attempted to duplicate the devil's handiwork. The resulting composition is considered to be Tartini's best work, as well as a musical monument to the power of dreams.

The Astonishing Night Journey

Some dreams are forgotten on awaking; others are powerful enough to haunt the dreamer for a lifetime; and—once in a very great while—there occurs a dream so luminous and profound that millions of people are inspired by its wisdom. Such a transcendent night vision came to the prophet Muhammad on a midsummer's evening in AD 620, eight years after he began to teach the new religion of Islam. The Isra and the Miraj, or the Night Journey, as the vision has come to be called, began in the holy city of Mecca when the archangel Gabriel appeared to the sleeping Muhammad *(above)*. "God commands you to come before His Majesty," Gabriel announced. "The door to the Seven Heavens is open and the angels are waiting for you."

Thus Muhammad embarked on a momentous journey that would take him into paradise and hell, as well as to some of the holiest places on earth. Before his odyssey ended, he would encounter great patriarchs and prophets of the past, view the wonders of the cosmos, and ascend to the very throne of Allah.

For more than a thousand years, Muhammad's journey has inspired poets and artists, who have tried to capture its meaning in words and pictures. The richly colored illustrations on these pages were discovered in a fifteenth-century manuscript, the work of three anonymous Persian miniaturists. Throughout the manuscript, the Prophet's head is shown surrounded by a nimbus of flames—a device widely used in medieval Islamic art to denote a sacred personage, much as a halo was in Christian art.

Following a ritual purification, Muhammad set out on the earthly portion of his journey, known as the Isra in Islamic lore. According to legend, the Prophet traveled on the back of a lovely beast called the Buraq, with the countenance of a woman, the body of a mare, and the hooves and tail of a camel *(inset, lower right)*. The Buraq, "whose every stride carried it as far as its eye could reach," was said to have borne other prophets to heaven, before the time of Muhammad. It became for some Muslims a symbol of love.

After making a stop at Mount Sinai, where Moses received the Ten Commandments, and visiting the tomb of Abraham and the birthplace of Jesus in Bethlehem, Muhammad rode through the skies surrounded by clouds of angels *(below)*. The multicolored wings of these legions filled the heavens like rainbows. Gabriel accompanied Muhammad on this portion of his journey to observe the wonders between heaven and earth.

In Jerusalem, Muhammad visited a mosque where he met an extraordinary group of prophets and holy men, including Abraham, Moses, and Jesus Christ. Muhammad counted Abraham as an ancestor; he traced his lineage to Ishmael, the son of Abraham and Hagar. In a prophetic gesture, Abraham invited Muhammad to lead the group in prayer *(right)*. The worshipers were illumined by seven hanging lamps. In Islamic tradition—and in some other cultures as well—the number seven is considered a felicitous sign, representing wholeness or perfection. The number was to appear again several times in the course of the Night Journey.

Fortified by prayer, Muhammad left the earth and began the Miraj, his ascent through the cosmos. When he entered the first of the seven heavens, which was rich in turquoise, he met Adam.

From Adam, Muhammad learned the secrets of time and duality, essential mysteries of nature to Muslims. Adam explained the paradox of timelessness in the midst of time. Muhammad observed the embodiment of this mystery: a great white rooster *(below, left)*. The rooster's feet rested on earth, where day follows night and seasons turn—firmly within the realm of time. His comb, on the other hand, reached high enough to brush the bottom of God's throne. At this extreme was a state of timelessness, of transcen-dence and the absolute. Gabriel explained that, at the hours of prayer, the rooster beats its wings and crows: ''There is no God but Allah.'' When other roosters hear this song, they echo it across the earth, calling the faithful to prayer.

As a lesson in duality, Muhammad was shown the descendants of Adam who were virtuous in life and those who had fallen into sin—their lots were, respective-ly, salvation and damnation, freedom and guilt. Muhammad also encountered an unusual angel *(below, right)*, made half of snow and half of fire, with prayer beads of ice in one hand and beads of flames in the other. According to legend, thunder heard upon earth is made by the col-lisions of these beads during devotions.

The second heaven was lustrous with pearls of wisdom. Here Muhammad was blessed by the prophet Zacharias and his son, John the Baptist. ''O Muhammad, welcome,'' they cried out, ''your presence honors the heavenly world. May the bounty of the Most High be yours.'' When Muhammad rose on the Buraq into the red hyacinth realms of the third heaven, he was greeted by legions of angels too numerous to count. One angel had seven-ty faces, each with seventy tongues sing-ing seventy exquisite melodies of praise for God *(right)*. Muslim tradition accepts this angel as a sign of God's omnipres-ence. The songs of glory that come to the angel's lips are samplings of the spiritual bounty that will reward the faithful.

Upon Muhammad's arrival at each of the next three heavens, he was greeted by an angel standing guard at the door, with thousands of others waiting in reserve to protect against the entrance of demons. According to the Koran, a demon trying to enter heaven would be instantly stoned or struck down by a falling star.

Finally, Muhammad arrived at the door to the seventh heaven—that composed of light—and was told Gabriel could accompany him no farther. The archangel unfurled his 600 wings and departed. Before entering the holy of holies, Muhammad bent to remove his sandals. God's voice stopped him: "O Muhammad! Do not remove your sandals, but let their blessed step attain my throne." The Prophet thus entered an ocean of light, and overcome with devotion and joy *(opposite),* he bowed to exclaim, "Glory and praise!"

The founder of Islam emerged from his encounter with the Divine carrying an edict for the faithful to pray five times a day. Reunited with Gabriel, he arrived at the gate to the gardens of paradise *(top, near left),* where angels welcomed him as an envoy of God. The gate through which the travelers entered was inscribed with the famous Muslim profession of faith: "There is no other god but Allah and Muhammad is his prophet." Within the garden, Muhammad encountered women of great beauty *(bottom, near left).* These were the houris, or purified wives, promised to Muslim men who led pious lives.

As Muhammad was soon to witness, however, not all humankind was destined for paradise. Still under Gabriel's guidance, he set out to tour the seven hells. In the first, Gehenna, he met Malik, the wrathful angel of death. On learning that the visitor was the prophet Muhammad,

the guardian of the underworld paid his respects, opening the doors of hell *(opposite)* and whipping the flames to a fury. Soon Muhammad was convinced nothing around him could escape the fires.

While still in Gehenna, Muhammad saw an immense tree called the *zekkum (below),* a kind of giant cactus. This infernal tree was profuse with thorns as sharp as spears. Its fruit was more bitter than poison and took the shapes of animal heads—pigs, elephants, and lions. On the branches of the zekkum, sinners writhed in agony. At its trunk, others were tor-

tured by demons who cut out their tongues, only to watch them grow back.

The Prophet continued his trip through the levels of hell, and he saw every manner of punishment. Adulterous women were hung by their breasts from hooks. The immodest were tormented by snakes and scorpions. Misers were encumbered by millstones hung from their necks, while hypocrites were shackled. There seemed no end to the terrible suffering.

Muhammad's night vision gave the faithful a dramatic glimpse of heaven and hell

and served as a warning of the unswerving justice of Allah. During Muhammad's time, no particular distinction was made between dreams and waking visions. Since then, some scholars have speculated that the Isra and the Miraj may have been a combination of both. Others believe that the Prophet was literally carried to heaven. Muhammad reportedly said of the experience, ''My eyes sleep while my heart is awake.'' Whatever the case, there is no denying that the Prophet's miraculous Night Journey is one the world's great spiritual treasures.

CHAPTER 2

Windows to the Unconscious

he house was a grand and ancient structure, two stories high, with a handsomely appointed salon on the second floor. A visitor wandered through the formal rooms, admiring antique tables with gilded trim, fine old chairs with brocade cushions, and walls adorned with precious old-master paintings. "Not bad," he thought, with an odd mix of satisfaction and wonder. Although he had never been in the place before, somehow the visitor knew that the house and everything in it belonged to him. He descended a staircase to explore the ground level.

Here was a somewhat older setting with dark medieval cabinets set upon red-brick floors. Again, the visitor's sense of possession was strong. Swinging open a heavy door, he came upon a second stairway and followed it down to a vaulted chamber that seemed to date from Roman times. Stone slabs paved the floor, one of which was fitted with an iron ring. The visitor slid the stone aside and descended farther, down a flight of narrow stone steps. He now found himself in a low-roofed cave that had long ago been cut into the bedrock. The floor was thick with dust and littered with scraps of bone and broken pottery. Among these shards he discovered the crumbling remnants of two ancient human skulls, still partially intact. Upon making this find, the visitor abruptly woke up.

The "visitor" of this dream was none other than the famed Swiss psychiatrist Carl Jung, and the recollection of his sleep-induced meanderings struck him with the force of revelation. For some years, Jung had been searching for an overall theory of the human psyche—a master blueprint into which he might fit the complex and often conflicting elements of mind and spirit that make up the human personality. One of the most promising avenues of research, he believed, was through the analysis of dreams, so he avidly examined both his own nighttime fantasies and those of his patients. This dream, in particular, seemed to penetrate the very deepest recesses of the analyst's psychic being.

The dream came to him during a lecture tour in the United States, which Jung made in 1909 with his friend and mentor, Sigmund Freud. Jung had first become acquainted with Freud's writings nearly a decade earlier and had quickly become an outspoken admirer. The two men carried on a lively correspondence and met when they could to converse and discuss their work. Now both Jung and Freud were delighted at the opportunity to spend a stretch of time in each other's company. Like Jung, Freud was convinced that dreams shed light on the hidden workings of the mental process. His controversial book, *The Interpretation of Dreams,* had already become an indispensable primer for a growing band of doctors and psychologists who—along with Freud and Jung—were pioneering the infant science of psychoanalysis. Each morning of the tour, the two physicians would exercise their psychiatric skills by recounting their dreams of the previous night and comparing interpretations.

Freud's readings were always rigorously analytic. In Jung's dream about his ancestral mansion, Freud saw the house as a symbol of female sexuality. The bones and human skulls—well, their meaning seemed obvious: Jung's dream was clearly about death. Freud quizzed his colleague, probing and needling, and attempting to prove that Jung harbored a secret desire to eliminate two close female relatives. Freud demanded to know who they were.

For his part, Jung knew perfectly well that he held no such hostile feelings. But his relationship to Freud—in spite of its genuine warmth—was partially that of a disciple. He was reluctant to offend the older man. Perplexed, Jung eventually blurted out what he knew Freud was waiting to hear. The skulls, he professed, belonged to his wife and sister-in-law.

Freud grunted approvingly, convinced that he had successfully made his point. Jung, however, thought otherwise.

The house of his dream, Jung decided, could serve as a structural diagram of the human psyche. The second-floor salon, with its fine upper-class furnishings, represented the conscious mind and its store of acquired knowledge. Below lay the great uncharted realm of the unconscious, occupying successive layers, each darker and more alien than the last. As he descended from floor to floor, Jung saw himself reaching down into the depths of his unconscious mind. At the same time, he was turning back the pages of history, descending the ladder of human culture toward its remote beginnings. "In the cave," he declared, "I discovered . . . the world of the primitive man within myself—a world which can scarcely be reached or illuminated by consciousness." It was a region of primal importance, Jung believed, full of surging energy and untold psychic potential. He was convinced that if he could explore the cave he would find archetypal images that are the common heritage of all humankind.

Virtually every student of the human psyche since Freud and Jung's era has acknowledged the importance of dreams. But the way in which dreams operate—their causes, their function in a dreamer's mental landscape, and their ultimate significance—remains a matter of much dispute. Some, like Freud, believe dreams are manifestations of repressed desires, usually sexual in nature. To Jung and others, dreams are glimpses into a commonly shared unconsciousness and thus hold potential clues to personal self-realization. Still others see them as a psychic device for absorbing new experiences or casting off the frustrations of daily life. A few neuroscientists depart from such psychological interpretations altogether. According to this physiologically oriented school of thought, dreams are simply a mechanical reflex by which the central nervous system clears its circuits. As yet, however, no single theory entirely explains the rich variety of sensations and images that come to us in our sleep.

The first attempts to examine dreams in a scientific manner began in the middle of the nineteenth century. One of the very earliest theorists was Jan Evangelista Purkinje, a pioneer-

ing Czech physiologist who saw dreams as a natural restorative, releasing the psyche from its mundane workaday cares. "The soul does not want to continue the tensions of waking life," he observed in 1846, "but rather to resolve them." Thus each dream, with its kaleidoscope of fantasy and feeling, "creates conditions which are the very opposite of waking life—it heals sadness through love and friendship, fear through courage and confidence." Dreams, in other words, were the equivalent of escapist literature for the mind. A number of other researchers agreed.

Many others dissented, however. Among the most influential was French psychologist Alfred Maury, one of the first observers to study his own dreams in a systematic fashion. Maury set out to prove by rigorous self-analysis that dreams arise because of external sensations experienced by the sleeper. His approach to this study was to have a colleague sit at his bedside and—once Maury had nodded off—shine a light in his eyes, splash water on his face, or ring a bell in his ear. Maury found the results encouraging. When a lighted match was held under his nose, he dreamed about sailing on a ship whose powder magazine blew up. A drop of water on his forehead led him to a café in Italy, in midsummer, where he sat drenched in sweat and drank the wine of Orvieto. A whiff of eau de Cologne transported him to the Cairo bazaar. In one famous dream, Maury saw himself caught up in the French Revolution. He was condemned by a people's tribunal and carted off to the guillotine. At the dream's culmination, he felt the knife fall—then awoke to discover that a bedrail had collapsed on his neck.

Maury published his findings in 1861. Along with a description of physical causes of dreaming, he offered some intriguing opinions on the significance of dreams in relation to human psychology. As sleep begins to take hold, Maury sug-

The Austrian psychoanalyst Sigmund Freud sent a print of this 1906 photograph to a young Swiss admirer, psychiatrist Carl Jung. The two had corresponded for a year when Jung requested a picture.

Freud (front, left) and Jung (front, right) pose with other participants of a Massachusetts seminar in 1909. It was on this trip that the two began to clash over dream interpretations—including Jung's dream of a grand mansion, which he saw as a key to the human psyche while Freud insisted it symbolized female sexuality.

gested, the mind wanders and the powers of reason diminish. The sleeper enters a state that is comparable to senility or some forms of mental derangement. Like some very old men and women in their dotage, the dreamer regresses toward childhood. Memories bubble to the surface, and images of long-forgotten people and places crowd the mind's eye. "In dreaming," Maury declared, "man reveals himself to himself in all his nakedness and native misery." But what of the specific images found in dreams and the self-revelations that some believe they convey? Alfred Maury dismissed such considerations as empty and meaningless. Dreams hold no more interest, he wrote, than the noise made by "the ten fingers of a man who knows nothing of music wandering over the keys of a piano."

Most other investigators of this era tended, like Maury, to focus on the mechanics of dreaming. The German psychologist Wilhelm Wundt stoutly maintained that all dreams were physiological in their origins and that they resulted from the random workings of the central nervous system, which triggered memories locked in the cells of the brain. Wundt was founder of the world's first laboratory for experimental psychology, opened in Leipzig in 1879, and his words carried significant weight in his time. A contemporary, George Trumbull Ladd, who established the American Psychological Association, concurred and went so far as to suggest that dreams were hallucinations produced by the firing of nerve cells in a sleeper's eyes.

Nearly all well-known scientists in the second half of the nineteenth century held similar views. However, while there was widespread agreement on the causes, the functions of dreams remained quite a lively topic for speculation. A German researcher, Ludwig Strumpell, thought of dreams as a device for exorcising daytime cares—a kind of psychic bladder that excretes useless thoughts and emotions. Strumpell also echoed Alfred Maury in his contention that dreams work their magic by transporting us back to the lost paradise of childhood. Several other theorists of this era maintained that dreaming allows sleepers to enjoy pleasures generally denied them during the day.

Strumpell's countryman Karl Albert Scherner proposed one of the more intriguing possibilities. Writing in 1861, he suggested that dreams occur when a sleeper's sense of fantasy is allowed to run wild, released from the prim control of the waking mind. Why then do nocturnal fantasies sometimes assume such a grotesque and phantasmagoric character? Scherner's explanation was that dreams speak not in words but in symbols. If a dream shows a friend standing in the snow, for example, it might mean that the dreamer thinks of that acquaintance as coldly aloof. Scherner argued further that even those dreams that are triggered by bodily sensations are filled with appropriate images or symbolic equivalents. If a woman goes to bed with a headache, she may dream that the ceiling is crawling with loathsome spiders. Scherner contended that dreams often contain recognizable symbols for the parts of the human physiology. A dreamer's lungs might take the form of a roaring furnace, a clarinet or tobacco pipe might represent the male sex organ, and a narrow courtyard could symbolize a woman's genitalia.

Few other nineteenth-century researchers saw fit to venture into what was—for the time—such an alarmingly suggestive area. But even the staunchest adherents to the dreams-as-nerve-impulse school of thought allowed that our midnight visions could very well contain profound psy-

Amalie Freud (below) was devoted to her eldest child, her "golden Sigi." An attractive woman, she was the inspiration for Freud's Oedipal theory. Wool merchant Jacob Freud (right), posing with Sigmund in about 1864, also influenced his son. After Jacob died in 1896, Freud began examining his dreams and childhood memories, creating the basis for The Interpretation of Dreams.

ing decade of the nineteenth century, began his own exploration into the phenomenon of dreams, he did so against a backdrop of nearly fifty years of active inquiry and theorizing on the matter. Freud brought towering intellectual powers to bear on this fascinating mystery. And as the founder, along with his friend Carl Jung, of an entirely new scientific discipline—the practice of psychoanalysis—he would discover a particularly compelling need to understand the purpose as well as the meaning of dreams.

Freud was born in what is now Czechoslovakia, but he moved with his family to Vienna at an early age, when his father's wool business failed. Ambitious and studious even as a teenage boy, Freud was encouraged by his parents to pursue his educational interests. Later, they would sacrifice to send him to the University of Vienna. Trained as a neurologist at the university, Freud made some headway toward a career in research during the years immediately following his schooling. In need of money, however, he wound up opening a small medical practice in Vienna. At the age of thirty, he married Martha Bernays, the daughter of a distinguished German Jewish family.

Among Freud's patients were a number of young ladies who suffered from hysteria, a puzzling complex of symptoms that ranged from odd aches and twitches to debilitating partial paralyses. Unable to find organic reasons for these complaints, Freud decided that the causes had to be psychological. His patients' tics and phobias, he concluded, were elaborate defenses against the pain of long-forgotten psychic shocks, which they had experienced in childhood and which now festered in the unconscious. The cure, he believed, was to peel back the gauze of memory until the original trauma lay revealed.

At first, Freud would lead his patients back through

chic meaning. "The dream sometimes allows us to look into the depths and folds of our very being—mainly a closed book in states of consciousness," wrote F. W. Hildebrandt from Leipzig in 1875. And a few years later, the English psychologist James Sully declared that a dream "strips the ego of its artificial wrappings and exposes it in its native nudity. It brings up from the dim depths of our subconscious life the primal, instinctive impulses." As another British authority, Havelock Ellis, put it, in sleep "the fetters of civilization are loosened, and we know the fearful joy of freedom."

So it was that by the time Sigmund Freud, in the clos-

their recollections simply by allowing them to talk, urging them to ramble from topic to topic by a process he called free association. But before long he discovered that a quicker port of entry was through discussions of his patients' dreams. Each dream provided images that, upon analysis, would release a flood of buried memories, fears, and impulses. These, in turn, would lead back to the roots of the patient's difficulties.

Already Freud had made what he considered to be an invaluable discovery. Dreams have a use: They can be called upon to heal the psychic wounds that are sometimes at the root of mental illness.

At the same time that he was busily ministering to his patients, Freud himself was going through a period of intense uncertainty and doubt. Restlessly ambitious—and with a growing family to support—he found that the professional recognition he craved was frustratingly slow in coming. To complicate matters further, some of the methods he was developing and the ideas that his work was spawning were propelling him in highly unorthodox directions in the treatment of patients. Strange as it seems today, Freud's approach to therapy, in having clients rummage through their innermost thoughts and recount their most intimate memories, was highly provocative—even scandalous—for that time. Recurring bouts of anxiety plagued Freud's waking hours. It was as though he had taken on the psychic ills of all Vienna. "Inside me there is a seething ferment," he confided to a friend, "and I am only waiting for the next surge forward."

Searching for relief, Freud undertook a rigorous study of his own dream life. He found himself recapturing lost childhood memories, and the experience was not entirely pleasurable. He detected some of the same neurotic turns of emotion that trou-bled many of his patients, and he suffered through periods of depression in which he "understood nothing of the day's dreams, fantasies, or moods." By nature an assiduous scholar, he combed through the body of contemporary literature on the subject of dreams.

Slowly Freud began to weave together the diverse strands of his research and speculation. He would seize a thought from one authority, pick up a phrase from another, and apply them to an analysis of his own dreams. The ideas of Scherner, in particular, struck a resonant chord. Freud noted that in his dreams his anxieties were hidden in some play of fantasy and symbolism. Another authority to make an impression on Freud was Dr. Paul Radestock, a contemporary pioneer in behavioral research, who had drawn parallels between the visions in dreams and the hallucinations of mental illness. Freud embraced Radestock's suggestion that the eerie phantoms of both dreams and madness somehow relate to hidden, unfulfilled desires. The young Viennese physician even found merit in the theorists of earlier decades who had argued that dreams were primarily a response to physical stimuli. He observed that a salty snack of anchovies before bedtime would cause him to dream about water.

Freud gathers his family for a photograph in 1898 in the garden of their Vienna home. He was devoted to his shy, gentle wife, Martha, the woman shown here in the darker blouse. He was also close to the other woman in the picture, Martha's sister Minna Bernays, who came to visit and stayed the rest of her life. Minna displayed an understanding of Freud's work that Martha did not share; it would be echoed in later years by his daughter Anna Freud (front, center).

It was at this stately Viennese resort, Schloss Belle Vue, that Freud conceived of his theory of dreams as wish fulfillment. "In this house on July 24, 1895," reads the note that the psychoanalyst wrote to a friend, "the Secret of Dreams was revealed to Dr. Sigmund Freud."

Yet with all his study and analysis, Freud was struggling with the task of weaving a cohesive theory on dreams. Then one afternoon, on July 24, 1895, as he was sitting on the terrace of the hotel Schloss Belle Vue near Vienna, the solution to his problem became clear.

Freud was mulling over a dream of the night before in which he had encountered one of his patients, a young widow named Irma, at a family party. Irma had been much on Freud's mind in his waking hours. Her therapy had run into a snag, and she had gone off to her country estate suffering from spasmodic vomiting and other physical symptoms of her hysteria. Among Irma's guests in the country was a colleague of Freud's, a doctor named Otto. The very day before Freud's dream, Otto had returned to town and confided that Irma was "better, but not quite well." Ever sensitive to criticism, Freud took this remark as a slap at his professional competence. He was filled with anxiety over the matter.

Freud's sleeping mind took flight from there. In his dream, Irma approached and complained of terrible pains in her throat and abdomen. After scolding her for quitting therapy, Freud proceeded to examine her throat. He discovered a very peculiar growth on the walls of her mouth and throat and called upon a highly respected colleague to repeat the examination. This man, referred to as "Dr. M," was joined by Otto, and all the physicians remarked on Irma's affliction. Clearly, she was suffering from a very unusual infection. The dream resolved itself when it became evident that the cause of Irma's suffering was a careless injection administered by Otto for some earlier illness. Apparently, Otto had neglected to use a clean needle.

While Freud sat at the Schloss Belle Vue and pondered this nocturnal narrative, it suddenly struck him as terribly revealing. The dream was an act of revenge—against Otto for maligning Freud's ability, against Irma for resisting his clinical analysis. It was they, not he, the dream declared, who should be blamed for Irma's alarming condition. Even Dr. M came in for a rebuff, for the dream had pictured him as pale and lame, his usual authority diminished. In a moment of sleep, Freud had outfoxed his competitors and restored his professional pride. "The dream represented a particular state of affairs as I should have wished it to be," he later wrote. "Thus its content was the fulfillment of a wish."

Dreams as wish fulfillment—the thought would transform psychiatric history. This one missing scrap of inspiration enabled Freud to feel that he could move beyond the other scholars he had read in describing the meaning and importance of dreams. Freud's writings in this area would prove to be the foundation of his influential career. In a sense, therefore, the same insight can be seen as the foundation for all of Freud's analytic theories, and it would color the techniques of dream interpretation for many years to come. Freud later declared, "Insights such as this fall to one's lot but once in a lifetime."

There was still more gold to be mined in Freud's dream of Irma and her ill-fated injection. Minutely examining each image in turn, Freud focused on the chemical compounds contained in the syringe, the names of which had been revealed to him in the dream. One of them was something called propyl, and Freud deduced that his mind had free-associated this name with that of another chemical called amyl, an impurity in some cheap brandies. As it happened, Otto had offered Freud some very modest brandy only the night before. The second compound was trimethylamine, which had been described to Freud as a byproduct of sexual metabolism. The analyst detected numerous sexual references in his dream. The syringe, for example, was an obvious phallic symbol.

Although Freud's published analysis of his Irma dream covered many pages of closely printed text, he primly avoided pursuing the sexual clues that he believed to be contained in the dream. "I have not reported everything that occurred to me," he admitted in a single coy footnote. On the whole, however, sex was a crucial element, a cornerstone of Freudian theory. The hidden childhood traumas of his hysteria patients often turned out to be sexual in nature—possibly because his clientele consisted mostly of wealthy women in a sexually repressed Victorian society. Freud believed, however, that the same would hold true for the contents of any adult's dreams.

If so, the deeper implications of Freud's dream are not hard to find. As a number of present-day dream analysts have pointed out, Irma was young, vivacious, attractive, and unattached. Spurning Freud's advice, she had gone off to the country with another man. By the logic of dreams, both parties deserved vengeance.

Building on his notion of wish fulfillment and his instinct that consideration of sexual urges is paramount to any understanding of the human psyche, the Viennese doctor worked out an elaborate theory on the analysis of dreams. To begin with, he proposed that the source of every dream is an unfulfilled desire. Welling up from the unconscious mind, the desire troubles the sleeper and threatens to disturb his rest. But the sleeper wants to go on sleeping and thus imagines a story in which the desire is satisfied. "Dreams are the guardians of sleep," Freud declared, "and not its disturbers."

Freud also focused on the nature of unconscious desires. With children, he explained, desires may be entirely innocent—a special treat denied during the day, perhaps. Freud cited the example of his two-year-old nephew, Hermann. When the boy gave his uncle a basket of ripe cherries that he clearly wanted for himself, he dreamed of a cherry feast all his own. The dream wishes of grown-ups, on the other hand, Freud saw as fraught with disturbing sexual undertones and thus likely to take a more devious path.

Sexual urges are so repugnant to the psyche, Freud believed, that a mental censor, which he called the superego, was on the alert to squelch them. The sexual urges are not easily suppressed, however. They change their form, disguising themselves in metaphor and symbolism in order to elude the censor. Freud called this process dreamwork. A young man, for example, might dream of a knight in armor slaying a wicked king. By Freud's interpretation, the king is the young man's

Vienna (left) was Freud's home for most of his life, and he was part of the intellectual ferment that shook the city around the turn of the century. Patients flocked to his office, where they practiced free association on the sofa in his consulting room (top left). Afterward he would ponder his cases in his study (top right), which contained what he called little statues and images, including mythological figures; concentrating on them, he said, helped him to fix an evanescent idea. But the Vienna of his youth became increasingly hostile to Jews, as evidenced by the swastika that defaced the door of his home (above).

father, and the dream expresses both his urge to rebel and a guilty desire to murder his father so that he can sleep with his mother. But the dreamer's mental censor has cloaked this Oedipal scenario in the trappings of heroic saga.

Freud could find a sexual reading for almost any image that occurs in dreams. When an adolescent girl dreamed of a dagger or a snake or a stick or a church steeple—any long or pointed object, for that matter—she reveals her fear of and fascination with the male sex organ. Even the most innocent circumstances might be a disguise for forbidden impulses. A cozy house set between two stately mansions suggested to Freud a wish to engage in intercourse. Climbing a ladder referred to a state of mounting sexual excitement. Dreams of flying or of playing the piano both alluded to the rhythms of the sexual act.

Despite his sensitivity to the erotic undertones in dreaming, Freud was not of the opinion that all dreams have sex as their central topic. Missing a train he took as an optimistic sign, for the train stands for death and the dreamer could be thankful when it chugs off on its way. Other dreams speak of birth. On one occasion, Freud was treating a woman who had dreamed about diving into a lake "just where the pale moon is mirrored." In a highly imaginative interpretation, Freud decided that the dream was based on an elaborate pun on the word *lune*—which in French means "moon,"

and is also a French slang expression for the buttocks. He pointed out that many children share the misconception that babies emerge from their mothers' bottoms. He thus felt that the image of diving into the moon could be read as a symbol of emerging into life, because the symbolic actions in dreams often move in reverse. The dream thus showed that Freud's patient felt reborn—presumably as a result of his theraputic skill.

The sleeping mind often delivered its message by means of such feats of wordplay, Freud believed, and this talent, together with a tendency to make heavy use of symbolic imagery, was part and parcel of a process that he called displacement. Everything in a dream—people, settings, events—means something other than the obvious. If a young woman dreams of violets, as did one of Freud's patients, it may mean she is frightened of being "violated." Fears and desires that the dreamer refuses to acknowledge may be projected onto other people in a dream. Thus Otto, not Freud, became the villain of the Irma dream. Often, the most minor details will provide the most significant clues to the meaning of a dream. The analyst must therefore trace every image back to its origins, taking the part of a psychiatric Sherlock Holmes. Only then can the dream's facade be penetrated and the analyst move past what Freud termed the "manifest" content to discover the "latent" content concealed inside.

In an ominous display of anti-Semitism, Nazis burn Freud's books in Berlin in 1933. The psychoanalyst wryly observed that his works were blazing "in the best of company"—with those of Albert Einstein, among others.

A newspaper heralds the progress of an aging, ailing Freud as he makes his way from Vienna to asylum in London in 1938. In the photo he is accompanied by friend Marie Bonaparte and the U.S. ambassador to France. President Franklin Roosevelt and others helped Freud escape from the Nazis, who had ransacked his house, stolen money, and detained his daughter Anna.

free herself? And so Freud continued, chasing down the possible implications of his patient's dream like a terrier pursuing mice.

Freud puzzled over such problems of dream analysis for nearly a decade, refining his theories and examining more than a thousand dreams. Then in 1899, he published his masterpiece, *The Interpretation of Dreams.* Only 600 copies were printed, and those few took eight years to sell out completely. For his efforts, Freud earned the equivalent of $209. Although the book did not quickly find a wide audience, more than a few of those who read it and absorbed its wealth of insights were captivated and inspired. A coterie of pioneering young analysts fell under Freud's sway. Among this group, ardent and articulate, was the twenty-eight-year-old Carl Jung.

Working as health permitted, Freud wrote and saw patients at this ivy-covered house in London. At age eighty-three, fifteen months after leaving Austria, he died of cancer.

Compounding the challenge for the analyst is the dreamer's ability to condense an enormous amount of latent material into a single image or event. One of Freud's patients, an elderly woman whose marriage had turned sour, had a dream about an insect called a May beetle—better known in some parts as a June bug. Freud sketched the plot of this dream in three brief sentences, then followed with page after page of tightly reasoned analysis. He noted that the woman had been born in May and married in May; that the night before her dream, a moth had drowned in her drinking glass; and that her daughter, when a child, had stuck pins into butterflies to secure them in her collection. Was the dream a sexual metaphor? The May beetles certainly were, in Freud's opinion, for the dreamer's associations could be traced back to Spanish fly, which was supposed to be a powerful aphrodisiac. However, the killing of butterflies could also be construed as cruelty to animals. Perhaps the woman equated sex with cruelty. In her dream, the May beetles had been languishing in a box, and the woman had tried to set them free. Did she harbor a secret wish to be

Jung seemed handpicked by destiny to be Freud's disciple. All his life he had been subject to the most vivid and provocative dreams. As a child in a small Swiss village, the son of a parson, he had nightmares in which balls of light floated toward him like malevolent moons, threatening to engulf him. In later years, his dreams took on a visionary, almost prophetic aspect. When he came of age to choose a profession, he dreamed of an encounter with a magnificent sea creature, like a giant, tentacled shellfish, in a woodland pond. The round, luminous body of this apparition seemed to represent all the wonderment and poetry of the natural world. Jung decided then and there to concentrate in the natural sciences—a determination that soon led him to the study of medicine.

As a scholarship student at Basel University, Jung was beset by doubts and troubled by what he felt were conflicting aspects within his own personality. Once again, in 1895, a dream arrived to smooth the way for Jung. He saw himself struggling forward through a howling storm, in darkest night, with only a small candle to light his way. Gusts of wind kept threatening to extinguish the candle, although he carefully cupped his hand around the flame. Suddenly he felt an ominous presence behind his back. He spun around to face it and saw a gigantic black figure trailing him. Terrified, he awoke.

Immediately, Jung comprehended the message of his dream. The looming black figure was his own shadow, cast by the candle against the storm's swirling darkness. It portrayed the mystical, subjective side of his divided nature. And it seemed to be telling him something. Use the light of your conscious intellect, it seemed to say, to pursue your studies and move ahead in the world. But do not deny your shadow self. Even though it now frightens you, it possesses a deep and ancient wisdom. Jung understood that in time his shadow self would come to serve him, as he learned to integrate the two sides of his personality. A few years later, just such a process was begun—when Jung chose psychiatry as his medical specialty.

The young medical student accepted a post in a Zurich hospital in 1900, where his work with patients began leading him in the same direction pioneered by the master psychoanalyst in Vienna some ten years earlier. When Jung studied Freud's book, in 1903, he was struck by how closely it reflected his own ideas. "The interpretation of dreams," Freud had written, "is the Royal Road to the knowledge of the unconscious in mental life," and Jung wholeheartedly concurred. Over a period of years, he became a leading spokesman for the Freudian approach.

As time passed, however, Jung had opportunities to work closely with Freud and gained a deeper understanding of his theories. He began to question some of the older man's most important conclusions. Dreams were an early point of contention. One key Freudian precept was that the majority of dreams are symptoms of psychic illness, the neurotic outpourings of a troubled mind. To Jung this could not be further from the truth. He considered dreams to be as valuable and healthful as fresh air. Indeed, his own night fantasies had often proved to be a source of guidance and comfort. Jung found even more troubling Freud's emphasis on sex as the force underlying all dreams. And as for the Viennese master's definition of dreams as a form of wish fulfillment—well, that seemed at best to be no more than a partial explanation. "It is true that there are dreams which embody suppressed wishes and fears," Jung wrote, "but what is there which the dream cannot on occasion embody? Dreams may give expression to ineluctable truths, to philosophical pronouncements, illusions, wild fantasies, . . . anticipations, irrational experiences, even telepathic visions, and heaven knows what besides."

Within the framework of Freudian dream interpretation, such declarations verged on outright heresy. A break between the two men became inevitable. Their differences eventually came to the surface during a visit by Jung to Vienna in 1910. A conversation with Freud turned, as it so often did, to the role of repressed sexual trauma in the occurrence of mental illness.

"My dear Jung," the master admonished, "promise me never to abandon the sexual theory. That is the most essential thing of all. You see, we must make a dogma of it, an unshakable bulwark."

"A bulwark—against what?" Jung demanded.

"Against the black tide of mud"—here Freud paused, then grumbled—"of occultism."

Jung was, to say the least, alarmed by his friend's remark. He was put off by Freud's talk of bulwarks and dogma—ideas that Jung felt were contradictory to the process of freely forming scientific judgments. He thought that Freud was asking him to blindly defend the Freudian dictum on the preeminence of sexual urges within the human

*By age six, in 1881, Carl Jung was
already experiencing richly symbolic dreams, which
he would remember and interpret as an adult.*

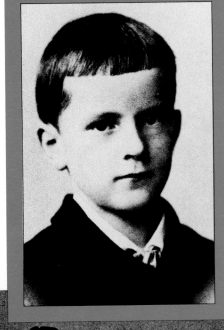

psyche—a theory that Jung regarded as little more than an untested hypothesis.

By "occultism," Jung took Freud to mean virtually everything that religion, philosophy, and contemporary studies of parapsychology had to teach about the workings of the mind. For a scientist, Jung was remarkably open to ideas from many different spheres of study. He had grown up in a family of psychics, where tables cracked and glasses shattered without discernable cause. His relatives held séances, his mother was subject to premonitions, and he himself enjoyed the investigation of arcane subjects such as alchemy and Spiritualism. How Freud's theory of sexuality would defeat the influence of these practices seemed not entirely clear. Jung knew, however, that his friend and mentor distrusted any excursion into the world of the spirit. To Freud, all such activities bore the taint of repressed sexuality—for that matter, so did many of the greatest works of art and literature. Jung, by contrast, saw these expressions as holding the potential to capture the essence of life itself.

Perhaps inevitably, Jung chose to part company with Freud. Between 1910 and 1913, he gradually made

Jung's parents introduced him to two subjects that would help shape his later work—mother Emilie dabbled in the occult, and father Paul was a minister of questionable faith.

more and more overt his misgivings about portions of the Freudian canon. Jung did so with considerable hesitation, because he shared with Freud a keen sense of the need to present a united front in the promotion of psychoanalytic theory. After all, the public at large and many within the scientific community were still openly hostile to the radical ideas of this discipline. The disagreement finally came to a head, however, at the Fourth International Psychoanalytic Congress, held in Munich in September 1913. At this meeting of practitioners from all over Europe, Jung and Freud faced off for the presidency of the congress. Jung triumphed in the election, but, in the process, he forced the membership of the congress to take sides, with bitter feelings all around—so bitter that afterward, Freud and Jung never set eyes on one another again.

On a personal level, the parting of the two friends and collaborators was extraordinarily painful for both men; so much so for Jung that he lapsed into a period of acute depression in which he felt himself near madness and kept a gun at his bedside in contemplation of suicide. For seven years, he was unable to accomplish any work, other

Images Bursting from a Brilliant Mind

Following his break with Sigmund Freud in 1913, Carl Jung entered a period of uncertainty that would last six years. During that time, he spent countless hours probing his own psyche, trying to decipher the images that bubbled up from his unconscious in uncontrollable thoughts, fantasies, and dreams.

Jung kept a record of his inner experiences in a folio volume he called the Red Book, re-creating the rich imagery of his visions in detailed paintings. This introspective work led him ever closer to an understanding of the unconscious.

The psychoanalyst's sometime guide on this quest was a fantasy figure by the name of Philemon, with whom Jung conversed and who represented, he later wrote, "a force which was not myself."

Indeed, Jung eventually concluded that many situations he encountered in his dreams and meditation had no basis in the events of his own life but had their origins instead in what he was to label the collective unconscious, the seat of inner experiences that he believed are common to all of humankind.

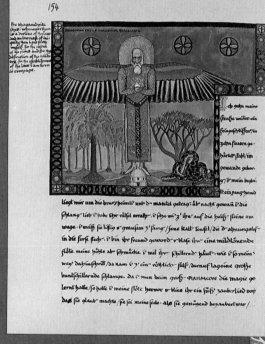

Jung painted the fantasy guide Philemon as a wise old man with wings. Jung's discovery of the sage inspired him to formulate his collective-unconscious theory. Philemon's presence revealed to Jung "the crucial insight that there are things in the psyche which I do not produce, but which produce themselves and have their own life."

This painting illustrates one of a number of dreams Jung experienced early in 1914, dreams he felt presaged the start of World War I. In this particular dream image, a divine or human figure hangs like a pendant from a large cross-marked disk. And the whole construct, ringed by flames, floats high above a landscape depicting scenes of war and technology.

A serpent rising from the heart of darkness is illuminated in this painting from Jung's *Red Book*. This dramatic image possibly represents the fruits of the quest for self while at the same time underscoring the psychoanalyst's thoughts about the duality of all things.

The dark figure in this painting represented for Jung the inferior elements of human nature, which he called the shadow. Acknowledging the beast within was a difficult but necessary task, Jung felt, in knowing the complete self. "The shadow is a tight passage, a narrow door," he wrote, "whose painful constriction no one is spared who goes down to the deep well."

In the vision that inspired this painting, Jung saw the Hindu god Brahma in serpent form, with the tree of life sprouting from its mouth. Unlike Freud, Jung recognized that other cultures, particularly Chinese and Indian, contributed to his theories, and he believed Brahma was "the star of the East, . . . the stag from the forest, . . . the end and the beginning."

than the creation of paintings that depicted his tormented dreams. Although Freud remained his usual combative self, he grieved in his own way—and perhaps in equal measure. Twenty years later, he would describe the rupture of his friendship with Jung as a tremendous loss.

When Jung had recovered his emotional balance, he set off to distill his own explanation for the complexities of the human psyche and to grind a new prism for the viewing of dreams. His search would carry him well beyond the closed doors of the psychiatric clinic and up through the wide open spaces of metaphysical speculation. In this pursuit, he could at times be disarmingly down to earth. "I have no theory about dreams: I do not know how dreams arise," he once wrote. But he never sold his subject short: "I know that if we meditate on a dream sufficiently long and thoroughly—if we take it about with us and turn it over and over—something almost always comes of it." And he would prove willing to follow his research wherever it led him.

Jung did have a theory about dreams, of course. He believed that they are messages—attempts to communicate on the part of the unconscious mind. Although he acknowledged the possibility that some dreams may be neurotic, he was certain that most are not. Jung saw dreams as capable of performing several practical and necessary functions: They are a relatively painless way for the mind to confront past experiences, to deal with present dilemmas, and to resolve all inner conflicts. He also felt that dreams were somehow akin to the musings of philosophers, inasmuch as they seek explanations for life's most basic mysteries. Moreover, Jung did not even believe that the process of dreaming was con-

fined to the hours of sleep. In his words: "It is on the whole probable that we continually dream, but that consciousness makes such a noise that we do not hear it."

In stark contrast to Freud, Jung believed that dreams communicate in a comparatively direct, straightforward manner. The nocturnal mind has no need to bury its insights under symbolic camouflage in order to slip them past the watchful eye of the superego. The censoring device described by Freud, Jung contended, simply does not exist. "There is no reason under the sun why we should assume that the dream is a crafty device to lead us astray," he declared. Dreams deal in strange images, to be sure, but only because the unconscious mind naturally thinks in terms that are archaic and visual. Jung argued that we are free to take these images at face value, without engaging in the narrow detective work of Freudian analysis.

A disciple of Freud might, for example, use the technique of free association to follow the clues in a dream about apples in a manner something like this: apples, pears, stairs, bedroom, bed, sex. But a practitioner of Jung's approach would find linkages that were even more flexible. The apple might call to mind a home-baked pie or a gift to one's teacher or food for thought or perhaps the tree of knowledge in the Garden of Eden. Any one of these associations might have a sexual content. Then again, it might not. Jung also defended the possibility that the apple might simply be an apple. More important than any single image, he maintained, was the dream as a whole and its initial impact on the dreamer. To illustrate this point he liked to quote a proverb from the Jewish Talmud: "The dream is its own interpretation."

In challenging Freud's concept of the superego as resident censor to the mind, Jung was attacking the very foundations of Freudian psychology. The Viennese master had divided the human personality into three unequal parts. The ego, or conscious mind, inhabits the world of daily life. Freud considered this our least important self. Above it sits the superego, spouting the dos and don'ts of our civilized upbringing. And underlying the rest is the great unconscious id—barbaric, untamed, insatiable, fixated on sex, and the ultimate source of all thought and behavior.

Jung joined Freud in ascribing great power to the unconscious sector, but he did not cast this portion of the human personality in a uniformly negative light. Although he agreed that the unconscious harbors its share of destructive urges, he also saw it as a realm of enormous potential and creativity. "Everything I know, but of which I am not at the moment thinking; everything which, involuntarily and without paying attention to it, I feel, think, remember, want and do; all the future things that are taking shape in me"—these for Jung were the contents of the unconscious. Even the awareness of one's own existence emerges from this part of our psyche, he said, for we wake each morning from the depths of sleep "like a child that is born daily out of the primordial womb of the unconscious." From this core issues forth the vision of the artist, the religious ecstasy of the saint, and the psychic forces that drive human beings forward to their highest potential.

According to Jung, the unconscious is a multilayered structure that serves as a storehouse for all kinds of instinctive, unarticulated wisdom. Near the surface lies a personal unconscious, which collects individual memories and repressions, much as in Freud's scheme. Then, at deeper levels, the unconscious embraces a more generalized type of psychic information. At bottom lies the collective unconscious, aswarm with images and impulses that are shared by all humankind. In much the same way that genes carry traces of the physical makeup of the earliest human generations, the collective unconscious contains memories and desires that may have had their origin in humankind's earliest experiences.

These primal memories, Jung suggested, repeat themselves the world over—in the myths and folklore of primitive cultures, in children's fairy tales, in the tragic dramas of Greek playwrights, in the symbols of witchcraft, in the rituals of church and state. They deal with the common denominators of human existence, such as birth, death, family, and the rites of passage from youth to maturity. The same motifs occur again and again, across cultures and throughout the centuries. A circle, for example, has always held special meaning—in general, it has represented unity. Jung called such a motif an archetype (pages 81-95), and he believed that each of us could gain strength by recognizing the archetypes that appear in our dreams and pondering their significance in relation to our waking lives. "All consciousness separates," he declared, "but in dreams we put on the likeness of that more universal, truer, more eternal man dwelling in the darkness of primordial night."

Another key element in Jung's psychic blueprint was the observation that, in waking life, people generally adopt a public demeanor with which to face the world. The cost to the individual of this emphasis on socially acceptable behavior is the neglect of the other sides of our personality. "Within each of us there is another we do not know," Jung declared. And how do we find these hidden aspects of our personalities? Jung counseled that they speak to us in dreams. A present day follower of Jung, psychiatrist Edward Bennett, tells of a punctilious bank official who dreamed repeatedly that someone was trying to break into his house. In every dream, the shadowy intruder would be moving from window to window, while the banker rushed about shutting each one. The door, however, was inevitably unlocked, and in the end the burglar would use it to enter the house—at which point the banker would wake up. By Jungian lights, the burglar was the banker's less restrained self, bent on breaking into and playing a role in the banker's life, which was sorely in need of leavening.

Jungian analysts take the view that experiencing a dream like that and then going through the process of interpreting it are usually sufficient to restore equilibrium in the dreamer's life. Often the key figure in such a dream is a member of the opposite sex. Jung accepted this as a reminder that all of us possess both masculine and feminine sides to our human nature. One of his patients, "a perfect gentleman," was repeatedly troubled by a nocturnal phantom in the form of an unkempt, drunken woman. Jung interpreted this unsavory figure as the patient's neglected female half—his anima—calling out for attention. He suggested that the dream was serving as a sort of psychic gyroscope for the patient. The man's unconscious was attempting to lead him to a more balanced—and, perhaps, less cautious—frame of mind. As usual, Jung was attributing a practical, restorative purpose to his patient's dream. It is likely that Freud would have discovered a much less benign explanation for such a dream.

The effort to find the meaning of dreams has scarcely abated in the years since Freud and Jung. Today, dream interpretation is widely practiced in the counseling chambers of psychiatrists, in the psychology laboratories of large universities, and in the bedrooms and living rooms of dedicated amateurs. New technologies have been enlisted to examine the sleeping mind, and new methods of analysis have been applied. Each month, scores of papers on dream theory are published in scholarly journals, and a great many articles on the subject appear in the popular press. In the midst of this continuing flood of interest and investigation, the basic discoveries of Freud and Jung, though repeatedly questioned, have never ceased to wield their influence. Even the severest critics of the two great pathfinders still must pay them deference.

The spiritual heirs to Freud and Jung in recording and analyzing dreams have staked out a wide assortment of programs for psychic therapy and self-improvement. The techniques applied in these programs vary greatly, but the premise behind them is generally the same—that dreams bring to light hidden attitudes and emotions, which may be obstructing personal fulfillment.

Among the most esteemed of the professional psychotherapists embracing this belief was Dr. Frederick (Fritz) Perls. Born in Berlin in 1893, Perls immigrated to South Africa with the onset of World War II and developed his ideas in relative obscurity, while living in that country. He published books explaining his theories in 1949 and 1951, but it was not until the mid-1960s, when Perls established a workshop at the Esalen Institute in Big Sur, California, that his influence began to mushroom. His approach is called Gestalt therapy. It holds, in part, that the way to attack a person's problems is not by rooting out long-forgotten traumas, locked in the depths of memory. Such Freudian concerns are set aside, so that patient and therapist can focus on the present. The current state of the patient's unconscious mind is what interests the Gestalt therapist.

Like Freud and others, however, Perls concluded that the best route to a patient's unconscious mind is through the person's dreams. "I believe that in a dream we have a clear existential message of what's missing in our lives," he declared. Working from this assumption, Perls and his followers devote a great deal of effort toward helping patients resolve the unfinished business brought to light in their dreams. The process has become one of the primary therapeutic tools of the Gestalt practitioner.

In Fritz Perls's workshops—which by the 1970s had cloned themselves across the length and breadth of the

In Search of Self

The crowning achievement of Jung's self-examination and his attempt to explain the unconscious, what dreams mean, and why people behave as they do was his concept of individuation. Jung explained individuation as "the process by which a person becomes . . . a separate, indivisible unity or 'whole.' " Dreams, he believed, play an important role in this process.

The key to wholeness, Jung said, is a "harmonizing of conscious and unconscious data." This involves allowing each aspect of the personality, such as the male side and the female side, to become fully developed. If any part of the personality is neglected and not allowed to express itself completely, the Swiss psychoanalyst theorized, it will find indirect and irrational ways to make itself known; in some cases, such misdirected expression could result in neurosis.

Jung believed that the personality expresses itself through an individual's dreams, fantasies, and delusions and that a person can only become whole by allowing all of the parts of the self to participate together in "open conflict and open collaboration." Since this dialogue is carried on in the language of symbols, however, it falls to one whose knowledge of the symbols is complete—the analyst—to conduct this process.

But Jung did note that individuation is sometimes aided by a means of self-healing that he felt can arise instinctively whenever it is needed. In

This mandala, drawn by one of Jung's patients, shows stages of individuation—from being entangled to gaining knowledge and, finally, illumination.

times of "psychic confusion and perplexity," he submitted, images called mandalas often appear spontaneously in dreams. And the mandala, Jung declared, "is the path to the centre, to individuation."

The word *mandala* means circle in Sanskrit, and in religious practices and psychology it denotes circular images. The circle, Jung theorized, imposes an ordered pattern upon chaos, "so that each content falls into place and the weltering confusion is held together." Jung believed that the mandala, which he referred to as the magic circle,

represents the goal of the self as a complete being and is a bold attempt "to see and put together apparently irreconcilable opposites." Just the appearance of mandalas in their dreams could have a healing effect on his patients, the doctor claimed.

According to Jung, a mandala is generally circular or egg shaped, and sometimes takes the form of a flower or wheel; often a square appears within a circle, or vice versa. And the circle's center point is usually marked by a star, a sun, or a cross.

Yet each individual's mandalas will also contain images that are drawn from an unlimited number of motifs and symbols that will uniquely express his or her own personality and experiences—and these symbols provide the tools for the individuation process.

Jung first dreamed of a mandala as a young boy, and he thought about the symbol constantly throughout his career. He was particularly obsessed with mandalas during his World War I military service at a camp for interned British soldiers; each morning he sketched in a notebook a mandala that seemed to correspond to his inner feelings. "With the help of these drawings," he recalled, "I could observe my psychic transformations from day to day." Eventually, Jung "acquired through them a living conception of the self," which he called "our life's goal, for it is the completest expression of that fateful combination we call individuality."

United States—groups of participants gather to read the messages in their dreams. The concept is influenced by Freud and Jung but differs significantly in that the psychotherapist does not assume that merely identifying a problem is, in itself, a solution.

Perls recorded the progress of a typical group in which a workshop member named Carl told of a recurrent dream. Carl recalled lying half-buried in a sandy desert, with the moon shining down from a blue-black sky. Train tracks stretched beside him, arrow straight across the desert floor. All at once, the dreamer heard a high-pitched whistle, and a train came roaring by. The train appeared infinitely long, its cars forming a never-ending chain reaching toward eternity. Carl was terrified. His thoughts gravitated toward death.

The analyst's response to this account was to launch into his own distinctive form of dream analysis and therapy. Carl was enlisted to perform an exercise in psychic theater, in which he plays the parts of every image in his dream. He first becomes the desert and quickly senses that it represents death. Next, he is asked to take the part of the train, and he describes his sensations like this: "I am a train and I'm going somewhere, but it's nowhere. . . . I have enormous direction, . . . but there's no home, no resting place at the end." Then, assuming the role of the tracks, he says, "I'm lying on my back and life is running over me."

Carl's sense of despair in this fantasy comes through with utmost clarity, but the therapist brings the playacting around to a point where the dream seems to point the way to a possible resolution. Instructed by Perls to improvise a dialogue between the train and the tracks, Carl discovers in a roundabout manner that the train brings to mind his mother. She is—the group learns—a powerful, overly controlling parent. When Carl carries on with the improvisation, he winds up shouting words that he longs to say to his mother. He tells her that she needs to accept him as he is and allow him to lead his own life. Thus, in the course of the exercise, the message of the dream has been made manifest: Carl has an unconscious desire to break away from his mother and assert his own personality. Perls would contend that the dream itself had already begun to loosen the parental bonds for his patient, but the additional work performed in the group has also helped Carl find the will to demand his independence.

Today, psychologists of various persuasions use techniques of dream analysis similar to those of Fritz Perls. In most cases, they will tailor the exercises to suit their particular approach to therapy. Another practitioner interested in dreams who has been influential in recent years is Mon-

tague Ullman of the Albert Einstein College of Medicine in New York. Building on a career of research in psychology labs and counseling clinics, Ullman arrived at an interesting theory on the function of dreaming.

Ullman believes the dreaming process was shaped in an era long ago, when humans slept in the wild—as most animals do today. In that time, dreams played a role in guarding human survival by alerting sleepers to possible danger. Ullman gives the example of an animal bedding down in its natural habitat. As the animal sleeps, some part of its mind must remain in a state of vigilance. The snapping of a twig or an approaching footfall can be a warning of imminent death. As the animal dreams, its mind takes in every sound and compares it to a store of sound memories. And in the event of a threatening sound, the dream will wake the animal up. Ullman sees this function carried over in humans in certain extraordinary circumstances, such as the soldier asleep in a trench on the battlefield.

Do-It-Yourself Dream Work

Freud called dreams "the royal road to the unconscious," and few experts would quarrel with the idea that dreams can reveal much about a person's attitudes, concerns, and anxieties. Remembering and examining dreams, therefore, can be of great benefit. Yet most people do not routinely remember their dreams when they wake up in the morning. Indeed, some people insist they never dream at all or do so only on rare occasions. Science has proved them wrong, however, with studies showing that everyone dreams and that we may have as many as four or five dreams per night.

The problem for dreamer and "nondreamer" alike is that our memory of dreams tends to evaporate quickly as time passes, beginning with the moment we awake. No one knows for sure why this happens; scientists speculate the process of forgetting begins even while the dream is in progress, so that any dream memory is only of the most recent dream action.

One antidote to this ongoing loss of dream memory is to keep a dream journal. The journal can be a notebook or a tape recorder placed on a table next to the bed. Upon awaking, you can write down or dictate as much of your dreams as you remember, adding to the entry later in the day if more night images resurface in your mind.

Recalling your dreams. Before you can keep a successful dream journal, however, you may need help in jogging your memory. It helps to be patient when learning to recall dreams—you may have spent a lifetime ignoring dreams, and it could take days and even weeks to begin remembering them. One tip for sharper dream recall involves going to bed with a clear head; being too tired can cloud memory in the morning, and studies have shown that alcohol and drugs, including sleeping pills, taken before bedtime alter the time spent dreaming.

Experts also suggest allowing yourself some quiet, reflective moments upon awaking. Lie still, keep your eyes closed, and relax. Then ask yourself, "What was I just dreaming?" You may only remember a fragment of an image, but further memory sleuthing might lead back to a complete picture. With those images fresh in your mind, reach for the dream journal.

Recording your dreams. Sometimes the simple process of writing or speaking of your dreams triggers other images and details, so it is best to record dreams soon after waking. In fact, the process of recording your dreams can begin *before* you go to sleep. Some dream therapists suggest jotting down your thoughts and feelings about the day just prior to bedtime. This not only helps you become more comfortable with the journal-writing process; these notes may also help you see how your dreams correspond to what you experienced during the day.

When recording an actual dream, do not stop to think of what it might mean; just concentrate on getting down the dream's plot. Try to recall details of places or characters, but do not struggle for precise descriptions—you can go back afterward and fill in particulars or nuances, impressions or emotions. Also record any fantasies, quotes, songs, and poems that appeared; you might want to sketch or paint your dream images so that you can study them from time to time.

In reconstructing your dreams, do not try to shoehorn them into the mold of reality. Logical sequences and cause and effect often do not apply. Accept the order of images and events as they seem to have occurred, and enter them that way in the journal.

Once you have finished, be sure to write down the date of the dream and, if you can, the approximate time it took place. Dream fragments may come back to you later in the day or even a few days later; record them in the margin beside the original entry.

Sometimes images appear over and over in dreams—a house or a clock, for example. Many experts suggest assembling a glossary of such images, listing each symbol and any associations that come to mind, and how it appeared in each dream. These images may have some personal significance that will be revealed as you study them and their places in your dreams.

Meditating on your dreams. Carl Jung believed a message could be found in almost every dream if one took the time to examine it carefully. Current dream analysts are in agreement that focusing attention on a dream—even just taking the time to recall it and write it down—can often lead to a greater understanding of its meaning.

Practitioners also suggest you examine entries in your dream journal for recurring symbols, characters, or themes. Many believe each image in a dream represents an aspect of the dreamer's personality and suggest role playing each image. Free-associating about a puzzling dream element—allowing any other words, images, or ideas it evokes to float to the surface of your mind—sometimes produces a nugget of self-revelation as well. So may extending an unresolved dream—replaying the dream in your imagination and giving it a conclusion.

Dreams are a symbolic language emanating from the depths of the inner self; taking the time to think about them and their possible messages may provide valuable insight. One caution: If you find yourself emotionally disturbed by trying to recall your dreams or by examining their meaning, give up the attempt and seek professional counseling. In fact, some authorities believe true dream interpretation should only be pursued with the help of a trained professional. The messages of the unconscious can be upsetting or frightening, they believe, if revealed too rapidly or without proper guidance.

For many of us, in the well-guarded comfort of our bedrooms, the most immediate dangers in life tend to be psychological. Apart from the threat of serious accidents or illness, survival is generally more of a social matter than a physical one. Have we offended the boss? Is our best friend annoyed? Will our spouses abandon us for someone younger and comelier? Ullman believes that the mind finds these sorts of "survival" issues to ponder in dreams. If it hits upon a particularly sensitive area, it stirs us into consciousness so that, with luck, we can focus on the problem.

From this starting point, Ullman's theory takes a decidedly Jungian slant. The stores of material in our cerebral data banks include, among other things, a number of personal myths or archetypes. According to Ullman, these myths are simply the ingrained patterns of thought that we unconsciously employ to cope with the reality of our waking lives. Almost every experience goes into this brew, from the carefully instilled lessons of our upbringing to the more haphazard images and stereotypes gleaned from viewing television. But as our lives progress and circumstances change, our personal myths have a tendency to lag behind. Ullman suggests that dreams may play a role in alerting us to the resulting discrepancies. They serve, says Ullman, "as corrective lenses which, if we learn to use them properly, enable us to see ourselves and the world about us with less distortion and with greater accuracy."

In Ullman's view, the most vivid dreams generally occur when our personal myths are beginning to change or update themselves. Often this occurs during periods of mental stress. Ullman cites as an example the sexual awakening of a commercial artist named Maggie. Shy and aloof in affairs of the heart, Maggie was troubled in her sleep by a huge, shadowy monster that appeared repeatedly to pursue her. When she turned to face it in a dream, the monster would disappear. One night, however, as the apparition faded from sight, she summoned up her courage and ran after it. When Maggie caught her tormentor, she screamed in terror—and at that instant the monster was transformed into a beautiful horse. She rode it up into the sky, whirling through banks of pink and azure clouds, and found herself in the embrace of a handsome man.

The meaning of this dream is readily apparent—at least in Ullman's estimation. The monster represents Maggie's adolescent instinct that sex is an ugly, fearsome thing. By means of the dream, her sleeping mind has succeeded in revising a personal myth, reshaping it into something more in tune with her adult needs. From that point on, Maggie's relationships with men took a turn for the better.

Ullman is of the opinion that because dreams deal so directly with social issues, they are best analyzed with a group of like-minded dream analysts. Only by going public, he says, does the dreamer benefit fully from the dream. In Ullman's workshops, a member will relate a recent dream, and the rest of the group will respond by describing how the dream makes them feel. The dreamer then weighs those reactions in a personal assessment of the dream.

As dream-analysis groups proliferate, people have begun to look for other uses for their nocturnal fantasies that go far beyond the narrow clinical role envisioned by Freud and the pioneers of psychotherapy. Dreams have become the raw material for a number of new programs and strategies for personal self-improvement. Artists and writers attend workshops on dreams in search of themes and images. Businesspeople scour their dreams in the hope of discovering answers to the problems of management and office relationships. At the same time, the role of the professional analyst in combing through the dreams of others is, at least for the present time, in decline.

Fritz Perls, founder of Gestalt therapy, believed a person uncovered his or her own dream symbolism by reenacting a dream and playing every role, since each reflected an aspect of the self.

"Once dreams belonged exclusively to oracles or psychiatrists," says a workshop devotee from Massachusetts. "Now dreams belong to the dreamer."

The trend toward do-it-yourself dream interpretation is propelled by such well-reputed gurus as Gayle Delaney, cofounder, with Dr. Loma Flowers, of the Delaney and Flowers Center for the Study of Dreams. A San Francisco psychologist and Ullman disciple, Delaney holds workshops, conducts seminars, and operates a telephone service that will help clients start their own dream-analysis groups. Her approach is eminently matter-of-fact. Sleep-time images, she declares, are a "reflection of your own mind considering challenges that you have been working on during the day." To focus on these various challenges, she advocates a technique that is called dream incubation.

The practice that Delaney teaches in her workshops is in some ways reminiscent of the "incubation" rituals held long ago by the Greeks in the temple at Epidaurus *(page 32)*. In Delaney's approach, the would-be dream incubator chooses a night when time is available to devote full attention to some important decision or a problem that needs to

be addressed. Before retiring for the night, the person spends a little time reviewing the plots and interpretations of dreams over the past few weeks, as recorded in a dream journal, and writes a paragraph or two outlining the events and feelings of the day. Then the subject mentally focuses on the topic that is under consideration, turning this idea over, examining it from every possible angle. At last, the dream incubator expresses the idea in the form of a single brief question: "How do I really feel about my job?" or "What is a good subject for my next painting?" Repeating the question like a mantra, the subject gradually gives way to sleep.

In Delaney's experience, many people can learn to incubate their dreams the first night they attempt to do so. Others may require a month or longer. For those who are really adept, she holds out the prospect of learning to control the course of their dreams, even while they are sleeping. With this capacity, Delaney believes, people will be able to open up completely new avenues for personal self-fulfillment. Such dream manipulation, or so-called lucid dreaming, as practiced by Delaney and others, has become one of the most exciting areas of research in dream laboratories today *(pages 110-113)*.

Although this new research is far afield from the theories of Sigmund Freud and might even have been a stretch of the imagination for the open-minded Carl Jung, it springs from the same conclusion that moved those two great pioneers. The pursuers of lucid dreaming start from the assumption that dreams represent the most likely way to tap the resources of the unconscious mind.

Beings from within Us

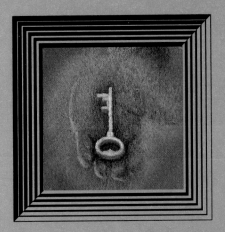

In addition to our immediate consciousness," wrote Carl Jung, "there exists a second psychic system of a collective, universal, and impersonal nature which is identical in all individuals." Inhabiting this collective unconscious, he posited, are what he called archetypes, the primordial images, or symbols, imprinted on the psyche at the beginning of time and since passed on to all humankind. The mother, father, child, and hero, with their associated motifs, are all examples of such archetypes, expressed the world over in myths, fairy tales, and dreams.

Dreams that present true archetypal images are rare, according to Jung. He found that they are likely to appear at pivotal points in a person's life, such as early childhood, puberty, early adulthood, midlife, before death, and at other times of crisis. Archetypal images in dreams, Jung held, give definite form to a particular psychic content of the unconscious, thus enabling it to enter the conscious mind. Professional analysis is usually required to interpret the full implications of archetypes. They often appear as symbolic images; the mother, for instance, might take the form of an inanimate object. But even if archetypal dreams are not understood, Jung believed, they would nonetheless "stand out for years like spiritual landmarks."

The dreams on the following pages feature several of the most common archetypes. Jerome Bernstein, a Jungian analyst practicing in Washington, D.C., provided these examples and much of their interpretation.

The Mother

Like all archetypes, the mother has both positive and negative connotations. In the following dream of a thirty-seven-year-old woman, the protective, nurturing aspects of the mother prevail:

"I was wandering through the woods, lost. I felt like Gretel in 'Hansel and Gretel,' but Hansel wasn't there to protect me. Suddenly I heard a rustling behind me. I was terrified and didn't dare move. Out of the woods came a beautiful woman. She seemed ageless. She smiled and gently pulled me into her lap. I knew that she was connected to nature and had magical powers. I knew that I would be safe. I had a strong urge to suck her breast. I was ten years old in the dream."

A dream of being lost in the woods, according to Bernstein, frequently symbolizes the beginning of a new phase of life and expresses the anxiety of leaving behind the familiar. In the case of this dreamer, she had just left a much-trusted female analyst to begin therapy with Bernstein. Her dread of working with a male analyst apparently stemmed from the fear and mistrust she felt toward all men. Her father had left home for good when she was ten—her age in the dream. And the cruelty she had felt from her mother during her childhood made her feel abandoned by both parents, much like fairy-tale Gretel in her dream.

The comforting mother figure in this dream—who the dreamer associated with her female analyst—indicates that the patient had healed the psychic wounds related to her mother. The appearance of this positive archetype, Bernstein says, signals that the patient is now ready to move on to the healing of the wounds that were caused by her father's desertion.

While the imagery in this dream is straightforward, the mother archetype can take several forms—both human and nonhuman. In its positive form, it may appear as a kindly mother, grandmother, or aunt, or as a church, a cave, or a garden. Associated with these images are maternal solicitude and sympathy, growth, nourishment, and fertility. Negatively, the mother may take shape as a witch, a dragon, or a shark and connote anything destructive and hateful, secret, dark, or hidden, as well as anything that devours, seduces, or poisons.

The Father

The father archetype commands center stage in the following dream of a fifty-three-year-old man:

"I was with another man, a shadowy figure. We went into a house. We saw an old man there. He was a former Mafia don. At one time he had headed the Mafia families. Now he was old, tired, and sickly. I realized that some time ago I too had been connected to the Mafia. Later, we realized that a contract had been put on the old man. We took pity on him and offered to help him, to help him hide out, to stave off his inevitable end. He insisted that we not do that. What would be, would be, he said. Finally the hit man entered the room. I pleaded with him for just a bit more time. The old man was ready, but I was not."

The significance of this dream reaches back into the dreamer's childhood, where he grew up in a sternly patriarchal household. As a boy and then as a man, the dreamer believed he had to deny his own burgeoning sense of masculine authority in order to not lose his domineering father's love and approval. As a result, he felt weak and ineffectual well into middle age. The emotions and memories unleashed by this dream, according to Bernstein, served as a turning point in the dreamer's life. He realized that the old man in the dream symbolized his father, who was willingly relinquishing his power so that his son might lay claim to his own. The dreamer interpreted the old man's insistence on not being saved as a sign he need not feel he was sacrificing his father's love by asserting his own masculinity.

Bernstein's analysis of this dream reflects Jung's view that the father as much as the mother plays a crucial psychological role in "the destiny of the individual." The power of one's father, according to Jung, derives from his embodiment of the father archetype. As an archetype, the father represents the ruler, lawgiver, or protector. It often appears in dreams as a king, an elder, or a heavenly father, or as heaven, the sun, a weapon, or a phallus. On the negative side, the father archetype may assume overbearing, devouring, or destructive qualities.

The Child

A depressed and angry forty-year-old woman had the following dream, in which the child archetype figures prominently:

"I was sitting on a bench in a park. It was a beautiful day. I was thinking about how I was going to accomplish all the things I had to do that day. Suddenly there was a little girl in front of me. She was about six years old. She radiated joy and happiness. She was dressed all in yellow. She said to me in a tone I absolutely could not resist, 'Will you play with me?' I smiled. She took my hand."

The radiant little girl in this dream, according to Bernstein, represents the arrested child within the adult woman. Her parents had divorced when she was six—the age of the little girl in the dream. From that point on, her mother treated her as if she were a burden, and little joy remained in the child's life. She grew into a somber and morose woman who had trouble with both her professional and private lives. The dream, says Bernstein, symbolizes her inner child breaking through from the realm of her subconscious to intrude upon her conscious frame of mind. By asking her to play, the child reveals the dreamer's desperate need to learn how to play again and enjoy life.

The dream above illustrates Jung's view that "the child motif is a picture of certain forgotten things in our childhood." Here, the dreamer had literally forgotten how to play. But, Jung continued, the archetype represents not only what has been but what can be. The occurrence of the child motif in a person's psychology, he wrote, "paves the way for a future change of personality." In the case above, as the dreamer set about learning to play, some of her unhappiness began to fall away.

In religion and mythology, the child-hero and child-savior—such as Hercules, who strangled two threatening snakes when he was a babe, or Jesus, who saved humankind from eternal damnation—are common themes. The child archetype may take the hero or savior form in dreams, or it may manifest itself as the dreamer's own son or daughter or as any other youngster. It may appear to be of exotic origin or may even appear surrounded by stars or with a starry crown. In its negative manifestation, it may present itself as the child of a witch, with demonic attributes.

The Anima

Just as both men and women's bodies inherit a mix of paternal and maternal chromosomes, so their unconscious minds, Jung believed, comprise both male and female elements. In dreams, this hidden, contrasexual aspect materializes as an archetypal figure of the opposite gender of the dreamer. The feminine character in men Jung termed the anima, and the masculine nature in women, the animus—both Latin terms that mean soul. The following dream, from a middle-aged man, revolves around the anima:

"I was walking down the street and saw an old house with a strange door. I felt compelled to open it. Inside, there was an empty room, with the opening to another room at the end of it. As I entered the second room, I saw something lying on a cot. It seemed lifeless. I went over and looked more closely. It was a beautiful woman in a long white gown. She opened her eyes and smiled and said, 'I've been waiting for you for a long time.' A golden glow seemed to surround her."

This dreamer had been involved in a destructive affair with a woman he found irresistible because, according to Bernstein, he had projected his unconscious female side onto her rather than focus on it internally. The woman in the dream symbolized his inner anima and the positive feminine characteristics—openness, spirituality, earthiness, creativity—he had been repressing. Her apparent lifelessness and then her words indicate that she had long existed as a dormant psychic potential deep within the dreamer's unconscious.

Jung assigned the anima archetype an extremely important role, that of guiding a man to the depths of his soul. Coming to terms with the anima—which may appear in dreams as a goddess, an elf, a mermaid, or any female persona—supposedly provides spiritual inspiration and a more balanced view of life. In the above dream, the anima seems to be offering the dreamer this opportunity. But, like all archetypes, the anima may take negative form as well, appearing in dreams as moody, irritable, and oversensitive—the stereotypical "inferior" woman, in Jung's terms. Its appearance may signal that those destructive characteristics are dominating the dreamer's personality and that he might need professional help in overcoming them.

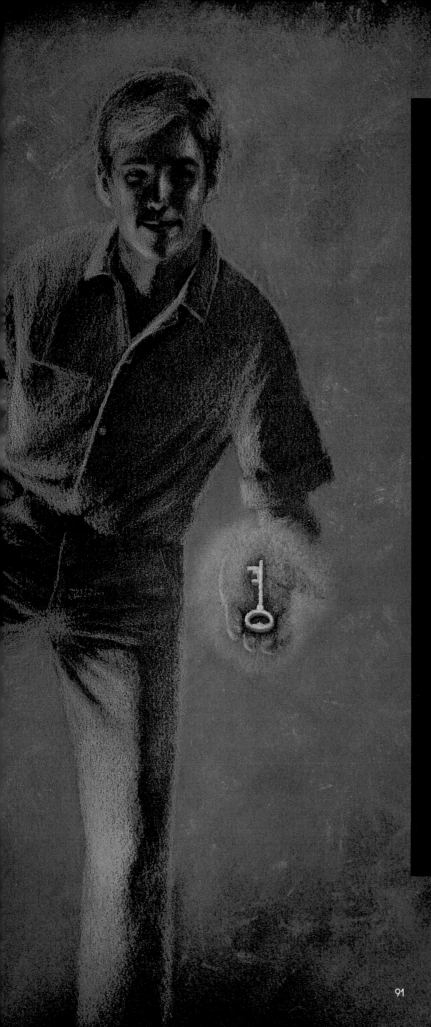

The Animus

The animus—the archetypal male figure that reflects the masculine principle in women—dominates this dream of a woman in her mid-thirties:

"I was sitting in my living room watching television. There was a fascinating man who was the husband of a woman in the drama. I thought to myself, 'I wish I knew someone like that. He seems to have such spiritual depth.' Just at that moment, he came right out of the TV set and walked right up to me. He didn't say a word but just smiled and handed me a golden key. He then turned around and walked back into the TV. I was astounded."

The dreamer, according to Bernstein, had been depressed for some time because she could not maintain relationships with men, who complained that they found her too hard and competitive. The attractive man emerging from the television in her dream, he says, represents her positive animus, of which she was previously unaware. And the golden key symbolizes her potential to unlock her inner mystery and find within herself qualities of great value. As the dreamer later explored her fantasies about the nature of the man in her dreams, she began to work at integrating into her personality the positive characteristics she felt he had projected, such as compassion and empathy.

A positive animus, then, serves much the same purpose for women as the positive anima does for men: Properly cultivated, it can open doors to inner wisdom and emotional and spiritual depth. Like the anima, however, the animus may also appear as an unfavorable force, the characteristics of which are also defined by cultural stereotypes of gender-appropriate behavior. A negative animus, in Jung's traditional view, causes a woman to be opinionated, argumentative, rigid, controlling, and excessively critical of herself or others. Its archetypal materialization in a dream might be taken as a warning that this negative masculine side threatens to rule one's nature.

Jung believed that there was a proper balance to strive for as regards the anima and animus. In general, the goal was to work toward integrating the positive qualities associated with them into one's consciousness and to guard against letting their negative aspects dominate.

The Hero

The hero archetype makes an abstract appearance in this dream of a timid, self-doubting male lawyer:

"I was on vacation, walking along a beach. I saw something sticking out of the sand. I looked closer. It was a torn and crumpled piece of paper. I picked it up. It read, 'Go to the land of your fathers. There you will find words.' It was an odd message. It made no sense. As I looked at it, I realized that if I took the *s* off the end of words and put it onto the front, it would read sword. At least the sentence made sense now, even if it didn't apply to me."

This dream shows the subtlety of dream symbols: The prescription for the dreamer's psychological ills was revealed through a seemingly trivial symbol—a discarded piece of paper. But what that scrap communicated, Bernstein explains, was that it was time for the dreamer to stop relying mainly on the intellect—words—and to claim the authority of the hero, as symbolized by the word *sword*.

Hero myths, common to all cultures, tend to follow the same formula: Born into humble circumstances, the hero soon exhibits superhuman strength, goes on to struggle triumphantly against the forces of evil, then often meets his death. The hero archetype reflects the sort of maturation process suggested by the myths. Its appearance reportedly signals the dreamer's awareness of his inner strengths and weaknesses, knowledge essential for the development of a healthy personality.

Although the hero archetype generally appears in dreams during adolescence and young adulthood, it may stay hidden awhile in the subconscious. The dreamer above, for instance, was thirty-seven. Over time he realized the heroic implications of his nocturnal vision—through his analytical work—and began to take charge of his life.

The hero motif may appear in dreams as a standard mythological character or as a modern-day hero, perhaps an athlete. Or it may take the role of an ordinary person acting bravely within the dream's context. When the hero continues to occur in an older person's dreams—a fifty-year-old man, say, seeing himself as a young athletic champion—it may signal that the dreamer is clinging to the illusion of youth rather than integrating a mature balance of power and wisdom. Women also have hero dreams, which are becoming more prevalent as women take on more assertive roles.

The Shadow

A thirty-three-year-old man who had been fired from his job for his role in a political scandal and saw himself as a victim related the following dream, in which the shadow archetype prevails:

"I was in a room, having a conversation with someone—I'm not sure who, it could have been me, too. I left the room, then for some reason turned back to reenter it. I opened the door and saw myself standing on the far side of the room. Looking to the left, I saw the back of another person. He turned around, and I saw he was also me. He seemed very startled to see me. As I looked at him, his face began to change into something quite grotesque—a monster-animal. I was horrified at the face of the monster and horrified to realize that all of these people I saw were different sides of myself. The person on the far side of the room saw my horror and said: 'I told you not to come back; you should have knocked before you came in. Now you know.'"

The shadow archetype, which is symbolized as the same sex as the dreamer, generally represents the darker, repressed side of one's character—the part most people choose not to face in waking life because it is inconsistent with their self-image. The dreamer above, for instance, saw himself as a doer of good deeds and blamed his troubles on others' persecuting him. This explicit dream revealed that unbeknown to him, there were unconscious sides of himself that were nothing less than monstrous. Up until then, the man had successfully hidden, or repressed, those destructive facets from himself. By exposing his shadow in all its awful truth, says Bernstein, this dream forced the man to accept responsibility for his actions.

Although shadow archetypes often appear in dreams as frightening or unsavory characters to be avoided, they can offer a dreamer useful revelations about his inner self, which he can then integrate into his waking life. Knowing that his shadow appears cold and forbidding, for instance, may encourage a person to be warmer and more compassionate in relations with others. True to archetypal form, a shadow may have positive as well as negative aspects. A meek person's shadow, for instance, may come across in a dream as a strong and assertive character who possesses qualities the dreamer might do well to assimilate.

CHAPTER 3

The Science of Dreaming

 keen-eyed graduate student at the University of Chicago observed something in 1951 that would dramatically change our understanding of sleeping and dreaming. Physiology major Eugene Aserinsky was studying the sleep cycles of infants when he noticed that during sleep the babies' eyes often continued to move under closed lids long after their bodies had become still. The eye movements would stop for a while, then begin again. Aserinsky thought that these movements might be a more reliable indicator of light and deep stages of sleep than the gross body movements researchers had previously relied upon.

Excited that he might be on to something important, Aserinsky took his data to his physiology professor, Nathaniel Kleitman. Kleitman speculated that the eye movements might also be useful in charting the sleep patterns of adults, whose brain activity could be electronically monitored at the same time. The two researchers quickly set up a sleep laboratory—a simple facility that consisted essentially of a bed, electrical recording equipment, and a technician to keep an eye on the sleeper and the hardware.

Two years of observation, first of Aserinsky's ten-year-old son and then of sleeping adult volunteers, revealed that sleepers had periods of rapid eye movement alternating throughout the night with periods when the eyes moved slowly or not at all. The investigators found that when their subjects were awakened from what was dubbed REM sleep, for the characteristic rapid eye movements, they were usually able to recall dreams in elaborate detail. Subjects roused from non-REM sleep, on the other hand, frequently could not remember even a fragment of a dream. Aserinsky and Kleitman discovered other differences as well. During REM sleep, the respiratory rate and heart beat sped up and were somewhat irregular. With the onset of non-REM sleep, both functions slowed and became rhythmical.

Aserinsky and Kleitman's 1953 report of their findings in the journal *Science* stirred widespread interest. Previously, sleep had been viewed as part of a simple continuum of consciousness, with very deep sleep at one extreme and highly alert states such as mania at the other. Many scientists had believed—but without benefit of experimental evidence—that a person typically fell into deep sleep a short time after dropping off at night; then, as morning approached, sleep would gradually lighten. Dreams were considered to be occasional, random events that tended to occur shortly before the sleeper awoke.

Now, however, it was clear that sleep was a far more complex phenomenon. From a rather simple observation, Kleitman and Aserinsky had made a radical departure in research, using physiological tools and methodology to study a subject that had for centuries been primarily the domain of philosophers and psychologists. Henceforth, scientists would be able to examine, from an empirical perspective, the ancient questions of when and why people dream.

Based on observations recorded in laboratories across the United States and abroad, researchers can now divide the nightly sleep cycle into several distinct stages revealed by eye movements and changes in brain-wave patterns as detected by an electroencephalograph. On the threshold of sleep's first stage, a transitional period between waking and sleeping known as hypnagogic state, the muscles relax and a person often experiences a sensation of floating or drifting. The eyes roll slowly and vivid images may flash through the mind—perhaps an eerie, unfamiliar landscape, a beautiful abstract pattern, or a succession of faces. As these sensations and visions come and go, a sudden spasm of the body called a hypnagogic startle may momentarily waken the sleeper. Then, as the subject slips into the first stage of sleep, the EEG shows the spiky, rapid alpha waves of a relaxed but wakeful brain giving way to the slower, more regular theta waves of light slumber.

Sleep's first stage is short, lasting anywhere from a few seconds to ten minutes. The theta waves soon decrease and are mixed on the EEG tracing with a combination of two different brain-wave patterns—groups of sharp jumps called spindles, which reflect rapid bursts of brain activity, and waves known as K-complexes, characterized by steep peaks and valleys. Although this stage is considered to be a true sleep phase, a person awakened from it may report having had brief bits of realistic thought or may even deny having been asleep at all.

Between fifteen and thirty minutes after the onset of sleep, large, slow delta waves begin supplanting the spindles and K-complexes of stage two. The change marks the deepest of sleeps, called stage three-four. (Many scientists divide this phase into two separate stages, identifying stage four by a yet greater increase in delta waves and a further decrease in spindles and K-complexes.) Waking from stage three-four is difficult. An individual typically feels quite groggy and disoriented and, even if an emergency demands alertness, must fight to overcome the compelling desire to fall asleep again. Talking in one's sleep, sleepwalking, and bedwetting tend to happen during this stage because of the brain's partial arousal from deep sleep.

After ninety minutes or so of sleep, most of it spent in stage three-four, the spindles and K-complexes of stage two briefly reassert themselves. The brain then shakes off the rhythms of non-REM sleep and passes into REM sleep—a condition so distinct physiologically from both wakefulness and the non-REM stages that some experts call it a third state of existence. Blood pressure and pulse rate rise, and brain waves quicken to frequencies comparable to those of

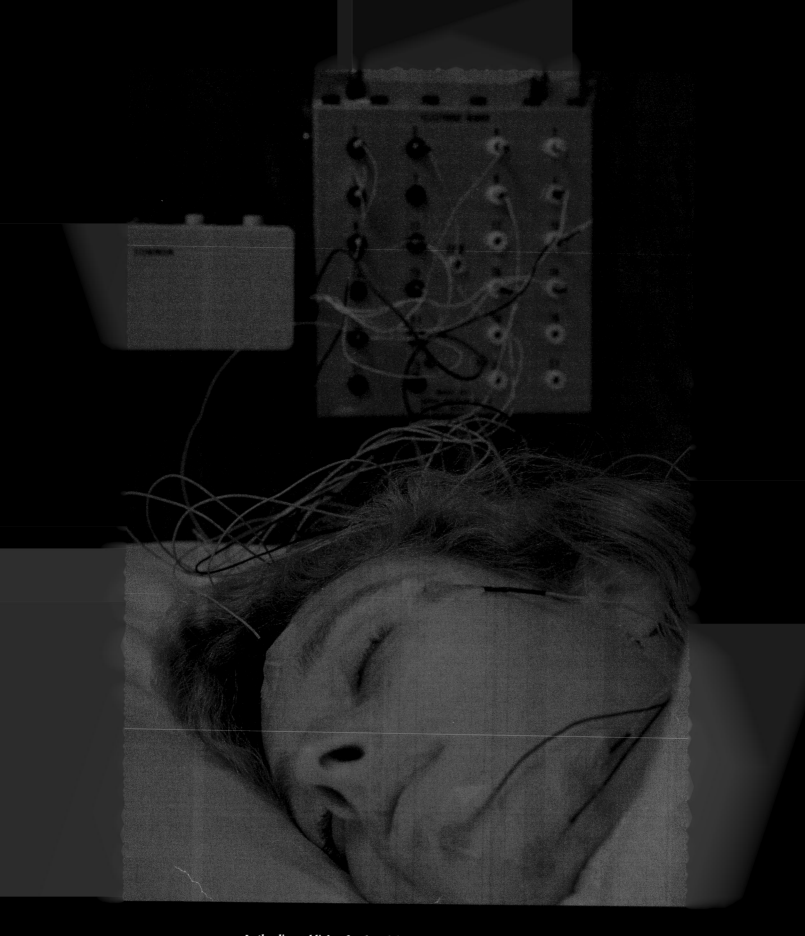

In the dim red light of a sleep laboratory, a volunteer subject slumbers with electrodes on her head and face. They detect brain and muscle activity, providing researchers with a record of dream-related phenomena.

an awake, alert brain. Yet, despite this activity, the body becomes remarkably still. The eyes begin their rapid movements, but otherwise, except for grimaces and small twitches of the toes and fingers, the muscles are temporarily paralyzed. In fact, a person awakened from REM sleep may even be unable to move for a few seconds. Scientists believe that nature has evolved this paralytic interlude, which seems to be controlled by nerve centers in the primitive brainstem, to protect the sleeper from the harm that might result if dreams were physically acted out. The two antithetical conditions of this state—a vigorously active brain within an immobilized body—prompted French neurobiologist Michel Jouvet to name it "paradoxical sleep."

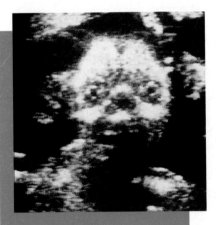

Most people roused from REM sleep will report that they were dreaming. While it is also possible to wake from non-REM sleep and recall images or thoughts that just passed through one's mind, these usually are akin to relatively mundane, everyday thinking and are quite unlike the vivid, dramatic, frequently fantastic images of REM sleep.

The first REM period of the night usually lasts anywhere from ten to fifteen minutes. Afterward, the sleeper drifts close to wakefulness before returning to stage two and beginning the sleep cycle again. (As the night goes on, stage three-four in the cycle may be skipped, and the sleeper will alternate between stage two and REM sleep.) Since each non-REM–REM cycle takes about ninety minutes to run its course, the average sleeper experiences four to five cycles per night. As the night passes, the REM periods become progressively longer—some lasting up to sixty minutes—while the time spent in the non-REM stages of sleep decreases. Consequently, almost half of a person's nightly dreaming often takes place during the last two hours of sleep.

All told, periods of REM sleep can account for about 20 percent of an adult's normal slumber. The average individual spends approximately four years of his or her life dreaming and can experience an estimated total of about 150,000 dreams.

Humans, and other mammals as well, appear to have a biological need to dream. This was first detected in 1959, through experiments conducted at New York City's Mount Sinai Hospital by William C. Dement, a psychiatrist and former student of Nathaniel Kleitman. For five nights in a row, Dement awakened volunteer subjects each time they entered REM sleep. He found that, with each succeeding night, the subjects entered REM periods more and more often until, by the last night, Dement had to awaken the subjects at least twenty times. Dement then allowed them a night of undisturbed sleep. As if hungry for dreams, the volunteers spent more of the recovery night than normal in the REM stage. By contrast, a control group of volunteers who had been wakened just as frequently but only during non-REM sleep did not increase their dream time during the recovery night. The tendency to make up for lost REM sleep suggests that dreaming is important for both psychological and physical health.

Dement's experiments also revealed some fascinating characteristics of REM sleep. He discovered a direct correlation between dream time and real time, laying to rest the common belief that dreams last only a few seconds. Volunteers' dreams usually took about as long to be played out as would comparable episodes in the waking world, as much as twenty minutes in some cases. A related revelation was that a particular sequence of rapid eye movements sometimes corresponds to the way dream images move. The eyes may actually track the dream's action, gazing about within the dream just as they would when watching an event in real life. In one remarkable instance, a subject was observed making about two dozen horizontal eye movements during REM sleep. He later reported that he had been watching a ping-pong game in his dream, and just before he had been awakened, the players had engaged in a particularly long volley.

Although Dement demonstrated the need to dream, exactly what causes those dreams to occur is still open to debate. One researcher, Dr. Ian Oswald of the University of Edinburgh, presents a purely clinical viewpoint, suggesting that dreams are the way the nervous system goes about repairing worn-out brain tissue. During non-REM sleep, Oswald found, various growth hormones pour into the bloodstream and course through the body, restoring bone and muscle cells after the day's wear and tear. But when the sleeper starts dreaming, the flow of hormones dwindles to a stop. Presumably restoration work then shifts to the brain, where raveled neurons and synapses are knitted up by means not yet understood. Dreams are the by-product of this activity, Oswald submits.

A number of other laboratory theorists follow similar lines of reasoning. Harvard Medical School's J. Allan Hobson and Robert W. McCarley, both of them psychiatrists as well as neurophysiologists, believe dreams arise because of nerve impulses coursing at random through a region at the base of the brain, where it meets the spinal cord. This most primitive area of the brain controls such activities as physical movement and the receipt of sensory impressions. During the dream phase of sleep these functions cease, rendering the dreamer virtually immobile. But the primitive brain keeps generating impulses on its own, say Hobson and McCarley, and emits bursts of meaningless neural static.

Some of these find their way to the neocortex, the site of most higher brain functions, including cognition. So the neocortex sorts them out as best it can, transforming them into shapes and colors and sensations, matching them with memories, building a story—and producing a dream.

Still other researchers speculate that dreams are the brain's way of keeping house. Among the foremost champions of this school are Francis Crick of California's Salk Institute, who won a Nobel Prize for his discoveries in genetics, and his British colleague Graeme Mitchison, a mathematician at Cambridge University.

Crick and Mitchison suggest that the waking mind is bombarded with so much information that its circuits are in danger of becoming overloaded. The particulars of life crowd in and register themselves in the neocortex. But the neocortex, despite its millions of interlocking nerve cells, has a limited capacity, and the overload causes confusion. Furthermore, most of the data it takes in is quite useless. Who needs to know the color of a matchbook cover, or the contents of the day's junk mail? So during dreams the brain sorts and organizes similar items. Not only individual bits of information but entire patterns of thought get swept into oblivion in a flurry of activity that the sleeper perceives as a dream. "We dream in order to forget," Crick maintains. But memories that the neocortex judges significant it retains, storing them in its network of brain cells for future reference.

The fashionable analogy for the brain's way of functioning likens it to a computer. The connections among brain cells are equated with the circuitry of microchips in a desktop or mainframe—a

Nathaniel Kleitman (left) emerges from a cave after a 1938 experiment with sleep cycles. This and other studies helped Kleitman show that sleep rhythms change with age.

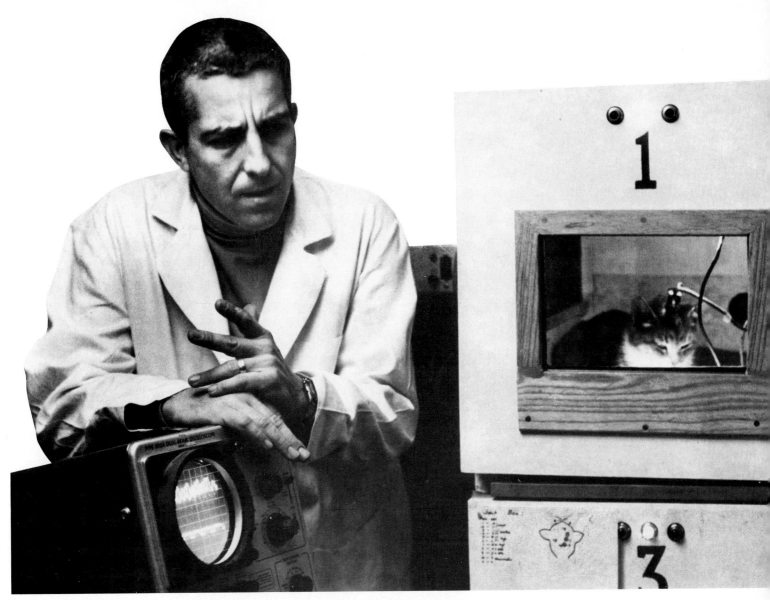

William Dement is pictured here with one of the cats he used for REM-sleep deprivation studies. Going without REM sleep for up to seventy days, the cats underwent behavior changes. Some became restless; others would not wash.

comparison that supports Crick's housekeeping thesis. But the analogy could also be used to argue that dreams may serve a more positive purpose. British psychologist Christopher Evans—who was also a computer scientist—explained how in his 1983 book, *Landscapes of the Night.*

While still a student, Evans was basking on a rooftop, cramming for exams, with his wristwatch beside him. Suddenly a hand reached through the open skylight, grabbed the watch, and made off with it. Evans chased the thief but could not catch up. So he hastened to the police station to make a report. What make of watch was it, the desk sergeant wanted to know. And although Evans had consulted his watch thousands of times, he could not remember.

That night Evans had a dream. He saw himself gazing intently at his watch dial. Its every detail appeared in vivid

closeup: hands, numbers—and the name of its manufacturer. It seemed almost as though the watch were signaling him, announcing its identity in a clairvoyant message from the world of stolen watches. But Evans had a different explanation. The needed information had been locked somewhere in his unconscious mind. Perhaps while we sleep, he reasoned, our brains sift through their cerebral data banks, and our dreams are reflections of this nightly browsing.

A similar function takes place in computers, Evans pointed out. Like the brain, a computer processes, stores, and retrieves information. But for maximum speed and efficiency, its operators periodically take the computer off line, shutting down its normal activities in order to scan through its programs, revising and updating them, and cleaning off extraneous data. Sleep is the brain's off-line period, Evans suggested, and the dream a kind of "memory filter," which sorts out the mind's accumulation of impressions and experiences. Some it retains in the brain's active file; others are consigned to a backroom storage area.

The updating process may occur during a single night or, for certain deeply entrenched patterns of thought, it may extend over many months. When Evans gave up smoking, for example, he began having nightmares in which he would find himself at a party with a lighted cigarette in his hand. Gradually, as his nicotine craving subsided, the dreams became less insistent and fraught with anxiety.

Other scientists have proposed that dreams serve as "sentinels of the night," periodically bringing the sleeper out of deep sleep so he or she can awaken quickly and respond to any danger that might have arisen. Another theory suggests that dreams are intimately connected to learning and memory. Studies have shown, for example, that after developing new skills in the day, people experience more REM sleep and slightly increased REM density—that is, their eyes move more rapidly—when they go to sleep. Conversely, the severely retarded have fewer dreams than those who are not mentally handicapped; their reduced ability to handle information, it appears, reduces their need to dream.

Dreaming may also serve as a mood regulator. After repeatedly being deprived of REM sleep, volunteers in laboratory studies are more prone to anxiety and irritability and have a hard time concentrating. Ernest Hartmann, professor of psychiatry at Tufts University School of Medicine and director of two Boston sleep laboratories, has proposed that the mental activity of waking life depletes the brain's supply of critical chemicals. A fresh supply produced during REM sleep, he speculates, helps maintain emotional stability and aids thought processes such as learning and memory.

But REM sleep is not always a restorative, and apparently there can be too much of a good thing. It has been found that some people who suffer from severe clinical depression pass through the initial stages of sleep to the REM phase more quickly, and stay there longer, than do healthy people. And unlike healthy sleepers, who dream most frequently during the last third of the night, depressed people may dream more during the first third, another indication of a malfunction in the body's natural sleeping rhythms.

Scientists cannot explain why such disturbances occur, but they have learned that a depressed person deprived of REM sleep for two or three weeks may find the feelings of despair and apathy lessening. In some cases, this simple therapy can be as effective as an antidepressant medication. A study conducted at the Georgia Mental Health Institute in Atlanta found that 50 percent of the subjects suffering from depression showed marked improvement after REM deprivation. (Those who did not improve also did not respond to medication.) The benefits of REM deprivation therapy, however, may be outweighed by its costs—the method requires a sleep laboratory and monitoring devices. But researchers continue to test the theory that the internal clocks of depressed patients may be flawed and are still experimenting with revised sleep patterns.

Besides establishing the normal nightly course of dreaming and some of its pathological aberrations, researchers have categorized two distinct but equally frightening disturbances: the nightmare and the much less common night terror. Everyone occasionally has a nightmare—a dream so frightening that he or she wakes up sweaty, short of breath, and with a pounding heart. Such dreams usually occur during the second half of the night, when REM periods are longer and dreams are more intense. Psychiatrists such as Stanley Palombo of Washington, D.C., believe that a nightmare (mare means goblin in Old English) dramatizes problems or anxieties one has recently encountered in waking life; in addition, it evokes related unconscious memories and images, creating an emotionally powerful mix. The feeling of utter helplessness that so often infuses a nightmare probably harks back to infancy, some experts say, when a child is indeed powerless and at the mercy of a world he or she cannot understand or control.

According to Professor Hartmann, "the common thread among those who have nightmares frequently is

*French neurosurgeon Michel Jouvet discovered that cats in REM sleep
lose muscle tone. He later learned that this is because the brainstem, the control
center for REM sleep, effectively paralyzes the body at the onset of REM.*

Turning his back on the remains of a recent meal, this relaxed leopard enjoys a nap. Some researchers believe it is in REM sleep that animals renew and reorganize information stored by the brain.

The Animal Experience

Animal sleep patterns are as diverse as the members of the animal kingdom themselves. Bats sleep up to twenty hours a day, while some antelope doze for just one hour out of twenty-four. And fish, which cannot close their eyes, appear not to sleep at all, taking their rest by simply not moving. Yet almost all mammals experience dreaming, or REM sleep.

Mammals are the only animals with a true cortex—the part of the brain associated with complex behaviors, including thought. Some scientists believe the evolutionary process that gave mammals their cognitive abilities also provided them with REM sleep as a means to process the information gathered by their highly developed brains. And that processing may take place through dreams.

If animals do dream, their fantasies probably lack the storylike structure of human dreams, which are based on language and our narrative manner of thought. But, as sleep researcher J. Allan Hobson points out, "mammals see, recognize, learn, and emote." Memories of these experiences, he submits, may surface during REM sleep, which may explain why a sleeping dog, for example, often whines and makes running motions with its feet as though it were chasing a rabbit.

Because the pace of the sleep cycle differs among animals—depending on such variables as body size and whether the animal is predator or prey—the number and duration of dreams also vary. A rat, though it may sleep for long stretches, shuttles between dreaming and nondreaming sleep every 6 minutes, compared with 150 minutes for an elephant. One theory holds that brain-activating dream sleep keeps vulnerable creatures from sleeping too soundly for too long.

The longest and deepest sleep, however, is probably dreamless. Hibernation, which allows an animal to survive low temperatures without food for weeks or months at a time, is a variant of the most energy-efficient phase of nondreaming sleep.

California sea lions pile atop one another on a communal sleeping rock near San Francisco. Safe from marine predators, the slumbering mammals can dream in the warmth of many bodies.

Two white-footed mice curl up together in their secure sleeping nest beneath a log. In addition to rapid eye movements during dream sleep, a rodent's paws and whiskers will twitch and quiver.

Fearing no other animals, this lion and lioness sleep with their vulnerable bellies exposed. After eating their fill in an hour, they may sleep—and dream—for most of the next two or three days.

Seen here at a polygraph he uses in research, neurophysiologist Hobson considers dreams a synthesis of jumbled memories. Each image conveys its own apparent meaning, he believes, and is devoid of any greater symbolism.

sensitivity." For a Boston study, he solicited volunteers who experienced nightmares at least once a week. A large number of the subjects were involved in creative work, such as art, music, and theater; others were graduate students, teachers, and therapists. Many saw themselves as rebels or as "different from other people," and some overtly rejected society's norms. "They were all very open and vulnerable," he said, traits beneficial to their careers. But "most had had stormy adolescences, sometimes followed by bouts with depression, alcohol and suicide attempts." Hartmann concluded that people who have frequent nightmares possess a poor sense of their own identities and find it hard to separate fantasy from reality. Some have borderline or potentially psychotic tendencies, he believes.

Night terrors differ from nightmares in both content and timing, and often occur in the deep slumber of stage three-four. The sleeper may rouse with a bloodcurdling scream and sit up in bed, terrified and confused, heart rac-

ing. He may also walk or talk in his sleep. While people usually remember specific and sequential details of their nightmares, the victim of a night terror recalls little or nothing of what triggered such extreme horror. Despite the severe panic it engenders, a night terror is short, lasting only a minute or two. (A nightmare can go on several minutes, but probably not longer, since the intense emotional state that results will often awaken the dreamer.) Night terrors seem to run in families, and researchers suspect they are triggered by a faulty arousal mechanism: Instead of following the normal shift early in the night from stage three-four sleep to a REM period, the sleeper partially rouses. Children are more susceptible than adults to night terrors, perhaps simply because they spend more time in stage three-four.

Whatever a dream's content, it reflects an altered state of consciousness that contrasts dramatically with the rational processes of the normal waking brain. In that respect, the dream state is like other altered states, such as those manifested during deep hypnosis, trances, and meditation, or through the use of mind-altering drugs. But dreaming is the most readily accessible of all altered states, the one that almost everyone enters naturally on a nightly basis.

Some psychologists are now exploring a fascinating, relatively rare state of consciousness called lucid dreaming. Ordinarily, a person knows that he or she has dreamed only after waking. But in the case of lucid dreaming, the sleeper is aware of dreaming as the scenes unroll before the mind's eye. Nor is the sleeper just a passive viewer—the most extraordinary hallmark of the lucid dream is that a person can affect the dream's events, characters, and emotional tone.

The earliest known reference to this phenomenon appears in Aristotle's fourth-century-BC treatise *On Dreams,* in which the philosopher states that "often when one is asleep, there is something in consciousness which declares that what then presents itself is but a dream." In AD 415, Saint Augustine recorded the lucid dream of his friend Gennadius. In the dream a young man discussed life after death at length and then told Gennadius, "I would have you know that even now you are seeing in sleep." Some eight centuries later, Saint Thomas Aquinas mentioned lucid dreaming. "Sometimes while asleep," he wrote, "a man may judge that what he sees is a dream, discerning as it were, between things and their images."

The first to methodically examine this aberrant type of dream was Marquis Hervey de Saint-Denis, a professor of Chinese at the Collège de France in Paris. His twenty years of dream research and analysis were summed up in the 1867 work *Dreams and How to Guide Them.* He said that good dream recall, the ability to will himself awake, and an awareness of the dream state had given him a measure of dream control, as his book's title suggested. Sigmund Freud himself praised the professor's research, and in the second edition of *The Interpretation of Dreams,* wrote, "there are some people who are quite clearly aware during the night that they are asleep and dreaming and who thus seem to possess the faculty of consciously directing their dreams. If, for instance, a dreamer of this kind is dissatisfied with the turn taken by a dream, he can break it off without waking up and start it again in another direction—just as a popular dramatist may under pressure give his play a happier ending."

Despite the endorsement of Freud and other respectable scientists, many researchers in the late nineteenth and early twentieth centuries joined the eminent English psychologist Havelock Ellis in discounting the idea of the lucid dream. Such skepticism prompted Dutch psychiatrist and sleep researcher Frederik Willem van Eeden to make public some of his findings on lucid dreams, first in fictional form in his novel, *The Bride of Dreams,* then, in 1913, before a group he hoped would be open minded or even sympathetic—Britain's Society for Psychical Research. One founder of the SPR, Frederic W. H. Myers, a highly respected Cambridge classicist, had himself succeeded in having lucid dreams on three occasions and believed that students of psychic phenomena should use these dreams in their investigations.

From his own experience, van Eeden was thoroughly familiar with the lucid dream—

Biophysicist Francis Crick theorizes that REM sleep evolved as a tune-up procedure for the brain, which allows unnecessary memories to be discarded. Trying to remember dreams, Crick says, may actually defeat their purpose.

a term he coined in his report to the SPR, in which he analyzed no fewer than 352 dreams. In lucid dreams, he said, "the re-integration of the psychic functions is so complete that the sleeper . . . reaches a state of perfect awareness, and is able to direct his attention, and to attempt different acts of free volition. Yet the sleep, as I am able confidently to state, is undisturbed, deep and refreshing."

Van Eeden purposely added an experimental element to his lucid dreams. In a September 9, 1904, entry in his dream diary, he notes, "I dreamt that I stood at a table before a window. On the table were different objects. I was perfectly well aware that I was dreaming and I considered what sorts of experiments I could make. I began by trying to break glass, by beating it with a stone. I put a small tablet of glass on two stones and struck it with another stone. Yet it would not break. Then I took a fine claret-glass from the table and struck it with my fist, with all my might, at the same time reflecting how dangerous it would be to do this in waking life; yet the glass remained whole. But lo! when I looked at it again after some time, it was broken."

The delayed shattering of the glass gave van Eeden "a very curious impression of being in a *fake-world,* cleverly imitated, but with small failures. I took the broken glass and threw it out of the window, in order to observe whether I could hear the *tinkling.* I heard the noise all right and I even saw two dogs run away from it quite naturally. I thought what a good imitation this comedy-world was. Then I saw a decanter with claret and tasted it, and noted with perfect clearness of mind: 'Well, we can also have voluntary impressions of taste in this dream-world; this has quite the taste of wine.' "

Van Eeden often had such lifelike sensations in his dreams. He remarked that "the sensation of having a body—having eyes, hands, a mouth that speaks, and so on—is perfectly distinct; yet I know at the same time that the physical body is sleeping and has quite a different position." He described the experience as "the feeling of slip-

ping from one body into another, and there is distinctly a *double* recollection of the two bodies.'' He admitted that Havelock Ellis would sneer at the idea, but these sensations suggested that he had what he called a dream body. Go-

ing one step further, van Eeden speculated that this dream body might be an astral body, an ethereal reproduction of his physical self. Although he was a scientist, he was ready to accept the possibility of a connection between the world of the occult and lucid dreams.

Van Eeden had little more success than the marquis de Saint-Denis had met four decades earlier in drawing scientific attention to lucid dreaming. If they even acknowledged the phenomenon, most researchers thought it an oddity at best. They believed that such an experience was not a dream at all but rather a ''microawakening,'' or partial arousal during dream sleep. Not until the 1980s, after Stephen LaBerge, a young researcher at Stanford University, established experimentally that a sleeper could alert observers to a lucid dream in progress, did the subject win a measure of respectability and serious scientific attention.

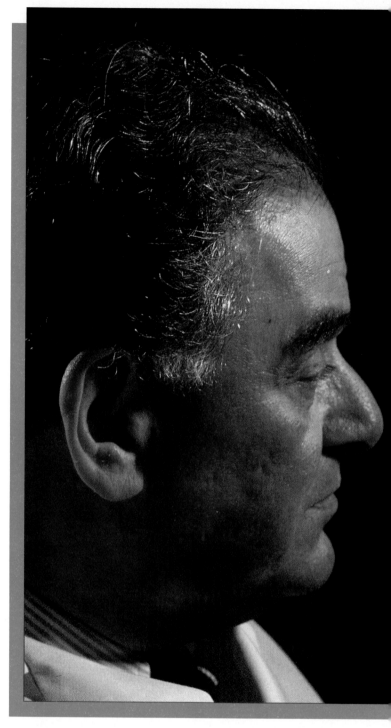

LaBerge claims to have had lucid dreams since childhood. During slumber, he would instruct pirates to return to his dreams night after night to continue their joint nocturnal adventures, and once, when he became frightened of drowning in a dream, LaBerge reminded himself that in earlier dreams he had been able to breathe underwater. Over the years LaBerge continued to have occasional lucid dreams, and in 1977, when he began work on his doctoral thesis in psychophysiology at Stanford, he decided to devise a way to study them scientifically.

An immediate problem was how to gather sufficient data—LaBerge experienced lucid dreams less than once a month. He first tried to increase the frequency of the dreams by using a technique of autosuggestion developed by psychologist Patricia Garfield—he would tell himself before re-

tiring, ''Tonight I *will* have a lucid dream.'' Using this method, LaBerge discovered that he was able to induce about five lucid dreams per month. By routinely reminding himself of his intention to be lucid during his dreams and by evolving his own technique, called Mnemonic Induction of Lucid Dreams, or MILD, LaBerge boosted his rate to more than twenty lucid dreams per month. On especially productive nights, he could induce four lucid dreams. LaBerge's procedure is fairly simple. After awakening from a dream, he memorizes its content, a practice intended to hone the abil-

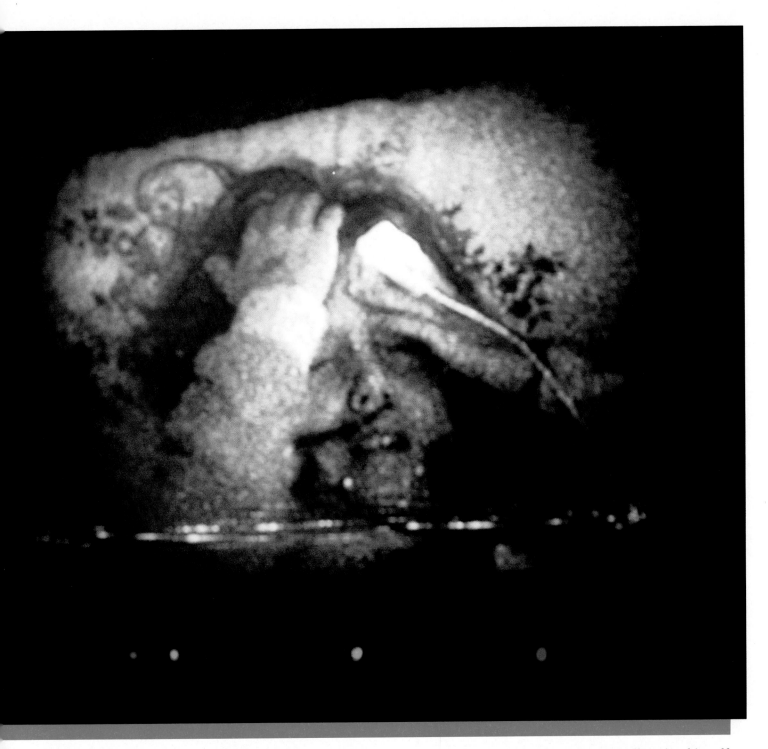

ity to recall dreams. Then, for ten to fifteen minutes, he reads or performs some other activity that demands wakefulness. As he is about to fall asleep once more, he tells himself, ''Next time I'm dreaming, I want to remember I'm dreaming,'' and imagines himself taking part in the dream he has just had, with the awareness that he is dreaming.

Intentionally inducing lucid dreams was LaBerge's first major research achievement. His second was to herald the arrival of a lucid dream by sending a clear signal during sleep, cleverly calling on the few muscles that are not im-

mobilized during the REM stage. Initially using himself as his principal subject at the Stanford Sleep Laboratory, LaBerge selected as his signal two vertical sweeps of the eyes. Each night he recorded his brain waves, eye movements, and the slight muscle activity of his chin and wrists on a polysomnograph (a type of lie-detector device). One night in 1975, after a series of tries, LaBerge examined the record of the previous night's session and found a telltale group of zigzags tracing the eye signal he had wanted to send. To prove that the eye movements were not REM related, La-

When Stephen LaBerge's eyes twitch in REM sleep, soft red lights in his goggles signal the advent of a dream. The glow does not awaken the "lucid-dreaming" experimenter but arouses him to take an active part in the dream.

Berge devised a second, more elaborate, signal to be sent by his clenched fists. In LaBerge's version of the Morse code, tightening his left hand equaled a dot and tightening his right equaled a dash. An electromyograph (an instrument measuring muscular activity) recorded LaBerge's predetermined message—his initials delivered in Morse code.

Frederik van Eeden had reported that most of his lucid dreams occurred between 5:00 a.m. and 8:00 a.m.—times coincident with longer REM periods—and LaBerge's work at Stanford confirmed his predecessor's experience. Color and light, according to van Eeden's report, are more intense and sensations in general are sometimes heightened in lucid dreams, compared with ordinary dreams. LaBerge and other contemporary investigators have gathered conflicting assessments of the sensory and perceptual content of lucid dreams, but on another point there is widespread unanimity—the lucid dream's powerful, mainly positive emotional content. Van Eeden's recollections are filled with words such as bliss, gratitude, piety, thankfulness, serenity, and calm. A contemporary of van Eeden, an Englishman named Hugh Calloway, reported that during his first lucid dream, "the vividness of life increased a hundredfold. . . . Never had I felt so absolutely well, so clear-brained, so divinely powerful, so inexpressibly *free!*" When a lucid dream does occasionally inspire negative emotions, they, like the more common positive feelings, are also unusually strong.

As a lucid dream draws to a close or lucidity fades, the dreamer frequently dreams of waking up. Such a false awakening can occur dozens of times within a single dream, and the lucid dreamer may go to great lengths within the dream to test whether he or she is still asleep. One subject reported, "I dreamed that my wife and I awoke, got up, and dressed. On pulling up the blind, we made the amazing discovery that the row of houses opposite had vanished and in their place were bare fields. I said to my wife, 'This means I am dreaming, though everything seems so real and I feel perfectly awake.' " But the dreamer could not convince his wife that it was a dream, so he decided to prove it to her by safely jumping out of their bedroom window. "Ruthlessly ignoring her pleading and objecting, I opened the window and climbed out on to the sill. I then jumped, and floated gently down into the street. When my feet touched the pavement I awoke. . . . As a matter of fact, I was very nervous about jumping; for the atmosphere inside our bedroom seemed so absolutely real that it nearly made me accept the manifest absurdity of things outside."

Lucid dreaming comes naturally to about 5 to 10 percent of the population. What traits these dreamers share is not yet clear, but researchers believe they may have identified a few. Jayne Gackenbach, an experimental psychologist at the University of Northern Iowa, found evidence that female lucid dreamers tend to be creative and adventurous during their waking lives—many of them relish such risky activities as scuba diving, rock climbing, and parachute jumping. And she suggests that both female and male lucid dreamers are less likely to be depressed or neurotic than the general population, although male lucid dreamers seem to be more prone to anxiety than their female counterparts.

Gackenbach and other psychologists report that people who do not spontaneously have lucid dreams can develop the ability if they are motivated and have good dream recall. Techniques such as MILD and presleep hypnotic suggestion and the use of special devices may aid the novice. LaBerge has designed plastic goggles with sensors that set off a pulsing colored light when the wearer enters REM sleep. The light arouses the dreamer just enough to make him aware he is dreaming. British psychologist Keith Hearne's compact device, which he calls his dream machine, uses a wire sensor clipped to the sleeper's nostril to detect the rapid, irregular breathing of REM sleep. The machine then sends four mild electric shocks to an electrode on the dreamer's wrist. The sleeper has been told in advance that the four shocks stand for a four-word sentence—"This is a dream."

Having the kind of pleasant, vivid experiences that lucid dreamers report seems reason enough to learn how to induce this type of dream, but there appear to be other reasons for bringing the notoriously unruly dream process un-

Drug-Altered Slumber

People have long sought artificial means to conquer the biological rhythms of wakefulness and sleep. Potions, pills, and liquor are all part of the pharmacopoeia and folklore of sleep. But their effects on sleep and dreaming are just beginning to be understood.

Amphetamines, which tend to decrease total sleep time, decrease REM sleep as well. But research shows that most sedatives, while inducing sleep and sometimes causing subjects to sleep longer, also tend to reduce REM sleep. Marijuana produces a similar effect, and alcohol just before bedtime suppresses REM sleep in the first half of the night; later, though, tipplers spend above-average amounts of time dreaming. With prolonged abuse in a constant dosage, REM-sleep disruption apparently decreases; however, drug withdrawal after chronic use often has a rebound effect. Some alcoholics studied just before and while experiencing delirium tremens (DTs), for example, spent most of their sleeping time in REM sleep.

Research shows that REM-sleep deprivation generally makes people anxious, irritable, and distracted. Definitive studies on the effects of drug ingestion on dream content are lacking, but a wealth of anecdotal evidence points to the powerful dream-altering effects of some drugs and natural substances. For example, LSD, mescaline, and some exotic mushrooms not only tend to increase REM sleep early in the night but can produce hallucinations—vivid dreams occurring in the waking state. In many cultures such dreams are part of religious ceremonies; certain Mexican tribes use peyote—from the mescal cactus—to induce hallucinations. The Huichol Indians often express their peyote-induced dreams in woven pictures called *nearikas;* the one above depicts a young boy on a quest for corn.

der some degree of control. Dream researchers see a variety of therapeutic possibilities. In fact, lucid dreaming is already being put to use to combat recurring nightmares. This technique, strictly speaking, is not an invention of sleep laboratories. More than two hundred years ago, Scottish philosopher Thomas Reid was plagued night after night by frightening dreams. Wanting to be rid of them, he decided that he would try "to recollect that it was all a dream, and that I was in no real danger." Reid began to remind himself before he fell asleep that whatever he experienced during the night would be only a dream. "After many fruitless endeavors to recollect this when the danger appeared," he recalled, "I effected it at last, and have often, when I was sliding over a precipice into the abyss, recollected that it was all a dream, and boldly jumped down. The effect of this commonly was that I immediately awoke. But I awoke calm and intrepid, which I thought a greater acquisition."

Whereas Reid performed an amateur's experiment, sleep researchers have devised more reliable methods to achieve the same end. At the Sleep Disorder Service and Research Center at Rush-Presbyterian St. Luke's Medical Center in Chicago, psychologist Rosalind Cartwright has taught patients suffering from a recurrent nightmare to press a buzzer when the dream begins. The patient is then awakened so he or she can discuss the nightmare with a psychologist and devise ways of changing its content. During the next visit to the sleep laboratory, the patient is again instructed to signal should the nightmare begin. This time, however, the lab technician does not wake the sleeper but instead buzzes back to remind him or her to change the dream. Using this procedure, one woman was able to rid herself of a recurrent dream in which she was being continually pulled under water by huge waves. She taught herself to dive under the waves in her dream—

"A bit like fireworks," wrote Marquis Hervey de Saint-Denis in describing the kaleidoscopic visions from the onset of sleep, now known as hypnagogic images. He included the drawings in his dream journal, which covered five years and filled twenty-two notebooks.

just as she knew she could do when she was awake.

Not all dream researchers count it wise to recast a nightmare and give it a happy ending. Psychologist Gayle Delaney argues that toying with a frightening dream may encourage a person to avoid the problems that inspired the dream in the first place. "Sometimes it's better that the dream end badly than to change it by being lucid." "If you awake frightened," she counsels, "you are more motivated to go and get help to understand what is threatening you, and then take the leap of courage to change your life."

Just as the unconscious churns up nightmares, it also processes workaday material and in dreams presents its own solutions. Throughout history, writers, scientists, and other creative thinkers have reported dreams holding unexpected and welcome insights. Athletes, too, have reported surprising revelations in their sleep. In his 1985 book, *Lucid*

Dreaming, Stephen LaBerge published a letter from a young hockey player who had been having trouble on the ice. She told of helping her skating technique by re-creating the experience of a lucid dream in which she flew effortlessly around the rink. "I brought back the quality of that dream experience into my wakened state. I remembered how I was feeling during the dream and so in the manner of an actor in a role, I 'became' the complete skater once again."

Professional golfer Jack Nicklaus, suffering from a long slump, credited a lucid dream with helping him regain his championship form. "Last Wednesday night I had a dream and it was about my golf swing," Nicklaus told a reporter in 1964. "I was hitting them pretty good in the dream and all at once I realized I wasn't holding the club the way I've actually been holding it lately. I've been having trouble collapsing my right arm taking the club head away from the ball, but I was doing it perfectly in my sleep. So when I came to the course yesterday morning, I tried it in the way I did in my dream and it worked. I shot a 68 yesterday and a 65 today and believe me it's a lot more fun this way. I feel kind of foolish admitting it, but it really happened in a dream. All I had to do was change my grip just a little."

People with a natural bent toward lucid dreams are also apt to experience vivid, kaleidoscopic images during the hypnagogic state, the drowsy interface of waking and sleeping. The body relaxes, blood pressure drops, and the heart rate and breathing slow. The individual may hear a cacophony of sounds—crashes, explosions, indecipherable voices or the repetitive calling of his or her own name—and experience a sensation of falling, accompanied by a hypnagogic startle; fragmented, nonsensical phrases may escape the lips. A hypnagogic episode may be accompanied by a frightening paralysis, and perhaps by a sensation of pressure on the chest, which can immobilize the sleeper long after the hallucinatory sensations have dissipated.

Although the episode is usually over in a few seconds, it may persist for several minutes, or even develop into a true dream. Severe fatigue seems to make people prone to hypnagogic imagery, especially when they have been deprived of sleep for twenty-four hours or more. And victims of narcolepsy, a condition characterized by uncontrollable sleepiness, frequently have such experiences, both at night and before dozing off during the day.

The images generated in the state are extraordinarily lifelike. A hypnagogic smell can propel a person to the kitchen to make sure that something is not burning on the stove. One woman who frequently heard church bells and organ music as she was falling asleep wrote that she "often got out of bed, opened all windows, etc., to ascertain whether they really were ringing, only to be met by complete silence outside." Some who experience hypnagogic imagery may feel as if parts of their bodies have become distorted or have disappeared altogether. Some researchers believe that hypnagogic sensations, particularly weightlessness and hearing voices, may somehow be linked to certain types of religious visions and out-of-body experiences.

Amorphous waves of color or clouds of diffuse light may mark the hypnagogic episode's onset and can gradually grow more complex. In 1912, Russian philosopher P. D. Ouspensky had a glittering hallucination. "I am falling asleep. Golden dots, sparks and tiny stars appear and disappear before my eyes. These sparks and stars gradually merge into a golden net with diagonal meshes which moves slowly and regularly in rhythm with the beating of my heart, which I feel quite distinctly. The next moment the golden net is transformed into rows of brass helmets belonging to Roman soldiers marching along the street below." Later in the episode, he flies from the window sill on which he has been lying. His senses are instantly heightened: "I smell the sea, feel the wind, the warm sun. This flying gives me a wonderfully pleasant sensation, and I cannot help opening my eyes."

Hypnagogic episodes are ordinarily pleasant, even comic. One imagist reported seeing a cartoonlike saber-toothed tiger, his paws held up to his face, tiptoeing on hind legs toward a victim who remained out of sight. Suddenly, the arm of a second striped tiger shot around from behind and covered the first tiger's eyes. Another sleeper described "a family of skulls in a car driving along . . . I could tell it was a friendly family." Yet every possible emotional coloration can be experienced in hypnagogic episodes. One dreamer described a terrifying scene that dream researchers find typical.

Dreams led chemist Friedrich August Kekule von Stradonitz to the structure of carbon-based molecules. Dozing one night, he saw dancing carbon and hydrogen atoms unite in a chain, the backbone of complex molecules. Years later in another dream he saw a ring structure and realized it was benzene—a discovery that launched the German synthetic-dye industry.

"I was lying in bed when I heard footsteps approaching my room. A prowler kicked open the door and strode to the bed, knife in hand. I wanted to leap out of the way, but I couldn't move a finger. I tried to scream but the sound was locked in my throat."

Although hypnagogic images occur most often as the subject is falling asleep at night, they can also develop as the sleeper awakes in the morning. At this hour, imagery is often the continuation of a dream. The sleeper's eyes may even have opened, but the transition to the waking state is not yet complete. In one case, the subject visualized a man he had just been dreaming about, standing next to his bed. "I looked at him for a second or two," recalled the dreamer, "and then putting my foot out, I kicked at him; as my foot reached him, he vanished." Another thought he saw an intruder squatting in his room. He jumped out of bed and grabbed the intruder—only to awaken fully and discover that he was wrestling with a linen bag.

The history of Western art is rich in anecdotes implying a link between hypnagogic imagery and creativity. Composers Johannes Brahms, Giacomo Puccini, and Richard Wagner, for instance, all said their musical ideas sometimes took shape during states of consciousness that a number of psychologists believe were hypnagogic. Nineteenth-century novelist Mary Shelley is said to have based her best-known work, *Frankenstein,* on horrifying hypnagogic imagery. And scientific and technological insights as well seem to have surfaced during such episodes. Thomas Edison was famous for taking a catnap whenever he became stuck on a particular problem. Holding little steel balls in both hands, he would drift off in his favorite chair. As his mind relinquished consciousness his hands would relax, droop, and finally drop the balls into pans strategically placed on the floor. At the noise Edison would jerk awake, often with an idea for solving the problem that had perplexed him minutes earlier.

A dazzling case of hypnagogic insight is said to be responsible for German chemist Friedrich August Kekule von Stradonitz's discovery in 1865 of the hexagonal ring structure of the benzene molecule. Unsuccessful with a problem he had been working on, he turned his chair to the fire and dozed off. Suddenly, he later reported, "atoms were gambolling before my eyes. . . . My mental eye, rendered more acute by repeated visions of the kind, could now distinguish larger structures, of manifold conformation; long rows, sometimes more closely fitted together; all twining and twisting in snake-like motion. But look! What was that? One of the snakes had seized hold of its own tail, and the form whirled mockingly before my eyes. As if by a flash of lightning I awoke. . . . I spent the rest of the night working out the consequences of the hypothesis."

The times at which hypnagogic images are most common are also the most favorable times for successful hypnopedia, or sleep learning. During borderline consciousness the brain is alert to outside stimuli; although it does not operate as efficiently as during full wakefulness, the mind often can absorb and retain information.

Sleep learning was first the stuff of science fiction. A novel serialized in *Modern Electronics* magazine in 1911 described a headband that transferred information from a central data store directly to a sleeper's brain via electrical impulses. Eleven years later, J. N. Phiney of the United States Naval School at Pensacola, Florida, devised experimental audio aids for drilling cadets in the Morse code during their sleep. It was in the Soviet Union, however, that the most important pioneering research was carried out. During the 1930s, Soviet psychoneurologist Abram Moiseyevich

Svyadoshch demonstrated that sleeping people could perceive and memorize straightforward facts and figures, such as foreign words and phrases or technical data; especially adept students could even master entire speeches in their sleep. His research seems ideologically neutral, but he was suspected of sympathy to Freudian thought, which was considered antithetical to the hard-line Soviet doctrine prevailing under Joseph Stalin. Not until after the dictator's death in 1953—by coincidence, the same year that Aserinsky and Kleitman announced their discovery of REM sleep—was Svyadoshch allowed to publish his findings. Some Soviet psychologists began to follow his lead in the 1960s, and their Japanese and Western counterparts soon joined in, swept along by the new interest in sleep phenomena.

Hypnopedia researchers soon established that effective learning is easiest to carry out when the brain is generating theta waves, which occur during the transition between wakefulness and sleep at the beginning and end of each night, and occasionally during the light sleep of stage one. Learning occurs when these theta waves are joined by alpha waves, which are induced by auditory stimulation. Attempts to instruct subjects during other stages of sleep have failed, but researchers say it may be possible to stimulate brain-wave changes during stage three-four to make the mind receptive to outside information. Until such manipulation becomes a reality, however, only about an hour of a normal night's sleep is available for sleep learning. Typically, an audiotape with a lesson lasting between three and eight minutes is repeated several times during each session. Just as in the daytime, students in sleep need more than one exposure to a piece of information to fix it in their minds.

Experiments have shown that sleep learning cannot replace daytime learning, but the two can sometimes be used in concert. Snoozing students can absorb facts—French verbs, mathematical formulas, historical dates—that are memorized by rote, but more complex learning requiring abstraction, analysis, and reasoning seems to be beyond the powers of the slumbering mind. Nevertheless, hypnopedia could be a real boon for students, adding hours of painless instruction that could speed their educational progress. Soviet researchers assert that months of hypnopedia produce no fatigue or other unwanted side effects.

Hypnopedia may be adapted to certain daytime applications as well. One laboratory, for instance, has taught people to use biofeedback to produce theta waves and thus enter and remain in the "twilight state" at will. This skill may be especially useful when learning is blocked by anxiety or other psychological problems. Thomas Budzynski, a Denver psychologist who is studying biofeedback, has reported the case of a graduate student who had failed a Spanish-language exam and was so nervous about taking it again that he could not study. Researchers prepared a Spanish-English tape that included soothing assurances that the student would be able to study effectively and remember the material. After hearing the tape twelve times while in the hypnagogic state, the young man was able to study without anxiety and passed the exam easily.

Sleep appears both to enhance learning and to aid retention of the information. Studies have shown that when subjects sleep immediately after memorizing facts, they retain more material—and can relearn it more easily after a twenty-four-hour lapse—than if they stay awake for a few hours after the learning period. Sleep, it seems, helps match fresh experience to related material the mind has already mastered and forges a link between the old and the new.

The shades of consciousness, from full engagement with the waking world to retreat into deep sleep's profound solitude, are being sorted out in ever finer gradations by researchers. They have traced the psychological and physiological paths human beings follow as they slip in and out of the world of dreams. But mysteries still abound. Scientists are left pondering what dreams are made of, and they pursue the answer with the most sophisticated of techniques and processes. Perhaps dreams will turn out to be nothing more nor less than the discernible activities of neuronal circuits. Or perhaps the study of dreams will ultimately force a look in other, more controversial—and less charted—directions for the missing pieces of the puzzle.

Dreams We Have in Common

Amid the kaleidoscopic swirl of unique dreams that emerge from each human mind are a handful that occur to almost all dreamers. Dreams of falling, being chased, soaring through the air, and losing teeth seem to be common manifestations of shared human experience. "Our dreaming self has apparently never lost sight of a basic truth," writes dream researcher Montague Ullman. "Namely that, despite the manifold ways in which the human race has fragmented itself in the course of history, we are, nevertheless, all members of a single species."

Some dreams are typical of a particular culture. The examination dream, in which the dreamer stares uncomprehendingly at a test paper, is a familiar expression of anxiety in industrialized societies. But the dream of being pursued spans cultural borders. The Masai may dream of being chased by an animal and the New Yorker of being stalked by a man with a knife, but the fear of being attacked is so basic that such dreams occur in almost all societies.

Yet even common dreams, each dramatically colored by individual circumstances, mean something slightly different to different dreamers. And as demonstrated by the typical dreams discussed on the following pages, each can be interpreted in a multitude of ways, according to various schools of psychological thought and dream theory. "There's no one answer to any of them," says psychologist Stanley Krippner, director of the Center for Consciousness Studies in San Francisco. "All of the explanations are all little pieces of the same puzzle."

The Fear of Falling

Almost everyone has at some time been jolted awake by the alarming sensation of falling from a great height. This unsettling phenomenon may be triggered by a dip in blood pressure, movement of fluid in the middle ear, or a limb dangling off the bed. But dreams involving a fall as part of a scene, such as tumbling off a cliff or out of a window, are nearly as common and seem to have deeper roots. Some psychologists speculate that they go back to when a toddler takes his first shaky steps, and the precarious sensation imprints the brain with an indelible metaphor for insecurity. Sociobiologists look back even further—to a primordial vigilance against tumbling from the tree while sleeping.

Whatever their cause, dreams of falling are powerful images that lend themselves to many interpretations. Sigmund Freud offered two. In women, he theorized, falling symbolized surrender to erotic temptation—the dreamer viewed herself as a "fallen woman." Otherwise, falling was an example of wish fulfillment, reflecting a desire to return to infancy when a child who fell was picked up and held in reassuring arms.

Psychiatrist Emil Gutheil suggested that falling could be a metaphor for the loss of equilibrium in many forms: loss of temper, loss of self-control, a falling away from accepted moral standards. Noting that such dreams are almost invariably accompanied by anxiety, Gutheil added that a pleasurable falling dream—one in which the dreamer drifts safely to the ground—should be classified instead among flying dreams *(page 127)*.

Contemporary theory holds that falling usually reflects insecurity—a sense that there is nothing to hold on to. People in the throes of a divorce or whose jobs are in jeopardy may dream of falling from a precipice. A child who overhears a quarreling parent threaten to leave home might have nightmares of tumbling into a deep hole. To men who fear impotence, falling can represent the failure to achieve an erection.

Sometimes, a falling dream can be taken literally. After dreaming of pitching off the balcony of her seventh-floor apartment, British dream researcher Ann Faraday found the guardrails on the terrace in need of repair—a fact she had not consciously noticed, but one that had apparently registered in the back of her mind to be brought out in a dream.

Finding Yourself Naked in Public

As recounted in Ann Faraday's *The Dream Game*, an unnamed university lecturer's recurring dream was an ordeal of public mortification: "He is walking through the college grounds or reading in the library when he suddenly senses all eyes upon him. Looking down, he discovers to his dismay that he is naked or clad only in shoes and socks."

To author Faraday, the scenario was a telling example of the common dream in which sleepers are embarrassed to find themselves in public either nude or wearing only their underwear. Such dreams often express feelings of guilt or inferiority. In this instance, the evident source was the lecturer's deplorable habit of pirating colleagues' ideas to advance his own career. Awake, he was cocky about getting away with his plagiarism. But the dream, which typically occurred whenever he published a new paper, expressed his deep-seated fear of being exposed as a fraud.

The traditional Freudian view of nudity dreams held they were inspired by an unconscious, infantile longing for the free, unclothed moments of early life. But today, dreams of public nakedness are considered more likely to indicate that a dreamer such as the one pictured here is metaphorically exposing what she believes to be her faults or that she feels vulnerable to some situation in her life. Such a dream may also connote honesty, expressing the sleeper's desire to strip away her facade and be seen for what she really is.

The tone and content of nudity dreams offer important clues to their meaning. For example, a dream of showing up naked at the airport the night before a journey might be no more than a reminder to pack underwear. If you are naked at a party or in the office, it can mean that you feel exposed to friends or co-workers. Clues may be found in the attitude of the other people in the dream. Disapproving onlookers signal guilt; indifferent ones may indicate that something you are concerned about revealing is not very important. In some cases, onlookers clearly approve of the dreamer, as they did in the case of one college student who dreamed he disrobed to the cheers of friends. The triumphant dream—which occurred soon after the young man had his first experience of sexual intercourse—was evidently a message that he was delighted with himself for shedding inhibitions.

Running for Your Life

The dream of being pursued or attacked—often accompanied by the feeling of being helplessly rooted to the spot—is common to all societies. In the United States, surveys indicate that attack/pursuit is one of the two most common anxiety dream themes among such diverse groups as college students, prisoners, and military inductees (falling is the other one).

Like falling, pursuit is a dream metaphor for insecurity. Yet people who dream frequently of being chased or attacked seem seldom to dream of falling, and vice versa, leading some investigators to speculate that the two dreams are flip sides of the same psychological coin.

The psychoanalytic tradition suggests that they represent two fundamentally different subconscious anxieties: fear of the loss of love in the case of falling dreams and fear of castration or, for female dreamers, sexual attack in the case of attack dreams. Another interpretation holds that a woman who dreams of being pursued is expressing a longing to be wooed. The fact that she is being "chased" is viewed as a punning reference to the word *chaste* and reflects contradictory desires to be courted and at the same time to maintain her virginity.

In the opinion of many dream researchers, this classic Freudian viewpoint is sharply limited. "It's good as far as it goes, and it explains a lot for some people, but it leaves out a number of equally valid explanations," states Stanley Krippner. Such explanations can range from the straightforward fear of being attacked by a mugger to a host of subtle manifestations in which the pursuer represents an unresolved aspect of the dreamer's situation or personality.

In *Working with Dreams,* Montague Ullman lists several questions that dreamers can ask themselves in order to explore possible interpretations of the pursuit dream: "Are circumstances closing in on you? Are you at the mercy of feelings that threaten to get out of control? Are you being victimized by someone else's aggression? Do you have feelings of guilt and a fear of being caught? Are you attempting to get away with something? Are you in the same position you were in as a child when you felt endangered by forces that were more powerful than you?"

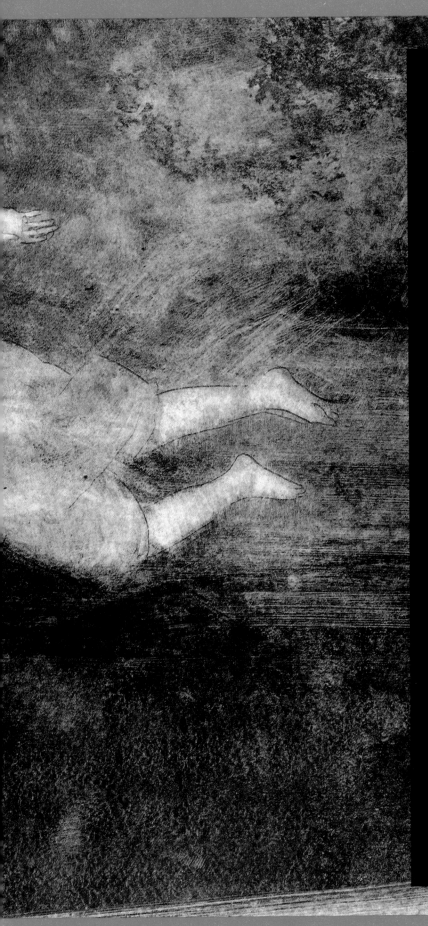

Taking Flight

Soaring through the air like a bird has been an intriguing feature of human dreams since ancient times. To the Babylonians, a man who took flight in his dreams would find riches if he were poor, freedom if he were a prisoner, and health if he were ill. Lydian soothsayer Artemidorus Daldianus said dreams of flying gave the dreamer a sense of elevation above others—as well as a promise of happiness and riches.

Characteristically, Freud saw sex in flying dreams—connecting the sensation of flight with orgasm and with sexual prowess. Because suspension in the air suggests ghosts and angels, Wilhelm Steckel, an early student of Freud's, linked dreams of flying with thoughts of death. Alfred Adler interpreted the dreams as revealing a will to dominate others, and Carl Jung believed they symbolized the desire to overcome a problem or break free of restrictions.

Contemporary dream research tends to ally itself with Jung's thinking. "People under a compulsion, people who are forced to endure unhappy circumstances (unhappy marriage, unhappy job or the like) experience their desire for freedom in their flying dreams," writes Emil Gutheil. "To fly then, means to be free." Bolstering such thinking is the fact that elderly people seem to dream of flight more frequently than do younger ones—apparently reflecting their desire to slip the bonds of increasing physical infirmity.

Flying dreams are generally pleasant, expressing strong feelings of competence or success. Television's Johnny Carson has said that he often dreams of flying and performing aerial acrobatics after having a good day at the studio—an indication that he "gets a lift" out of the verbal acrobatics he engages in when broadcasting.

Aside from traditional psychological theories, there is a school of thought that connects dreams of flight with out-of-body experiences. "It may be that we really are flying," suggests clinical psychologist and dream therapist Gayle Delaney, "albeit in another dimension of reality and perhaps in another body." According to Delaney, people who have learned to induce OBEs contend that if they become conscious while flying in a dream, they are aware of floating above their slumbering physical bodies in a second, astral form.

On Stage and Unprepared

In a recurrent dream that understandably unsettled him, playwright George Bernard Shaw found himself standing on a stage as the lead actor in a play that was about to begin. As the curtain rose, the master of repartee and biting dialogue realized to his horror that he had nothing to say. He did not know his lines.

To Emil Gutheil, who related it in his book *The Language of the Dream,* the nightmare revealed that the playwright—who in his waking hours was a man of fabled self-confidence—harbored a deep-seated anxiety about his ability to rise to the occasion when confronted with tasks to which he did not feel equal. To other dream researchers the dream might also have suggested that the great playwright subconsciously feared losing his prodigious verbal skills.

Whatever the interpretation, Shaw's dream, in which an inner drama of anxiety and inferiority is played out in a theatrical setting, is a typical variation of the even more common dream in which the dreamer sits down to take an examination, looks at the test paper, and realizes, to his horror, that he cannot answer a single one of the questions.

Such dreams occur with distressing frequency to students at exam time, when the meaning is starkly self-evident. But they also seem to recur time and again to adults whose school days are long over. Salespeople may dream of being examined or having stage fright the night before a sales presentation; athletes often have such dreams before competing in a sporting event.

In other cases, a dreamed exam or unprepared stage appearance is a metaphor for being put to the test on some personal issue. Noting that such dreams often occur at the "threshold of important decisions," Gutheil writes that they are frequent among those individuals whose self-confidence is at stake—a young man about to marry who doubts his sexual adequacy or his ability as a provider; someone entering a new job who is unsure of being able to handle new responsibilities. He notes that an examination dream may also signify a sense of being tested morally—"the 'final' examination as to one's 'good' and 'bad' deeds before the Highest Examiner."

CHAPTER 4

Psychic Dreams

hen he was a young man, aerospace chemist Edward Butler never put great stock in dreams, and he knew nothing of what are called paranormal or psychic dreams. But Butler experienced a dream in 1959 that he will never forget. That dream and its associated events have affected Ed Butler profoundly, and for the first time, in 1988, he shared it with the world on a television talk show.

The dream occurred when Butler was twenty-five years old, employed by a New Jersey company working in rocket engines and fuels. In the dream, he was sitting in his laboratory in his shirt sleeves, when suddenly a violent explosion shook the building. Rushing out, he discovered that an adjacent lab was ablaze and could hear screaming within. He dashed through the smoke and flames to find a co-worker named Rita Dudak burning like a torch, on fire from head to toe. Butler dreamed that he grabbed her by a leg and dragged her into his own lab, where he placed her under a safety shower, dousing the flames.

When he awoke, Butler pondered some curious details in the dream. It was strange that he would be in his shirt sleeves; because of hazardous experiments, lab personnel always wore fire-retardant coats when working. And it was odd, too, that Rita Dudak would be alone in her lab; three co-workers were almost always there with her. But Butler shrugged off the puzzlements and dismissed the dream.

But the dream would not go away. It kept recurring—not every night, but frequently and persistently, over a period of months.

Then it happened. On the afternoon of April 23, 1959, Butler was doing paperwork at his desk, and because he was in a safe area, regulations allowed him to be in shirt sleeves. Next door, Rita Dudak was performing an experiment with some highly explosive materials. She was standing behind two protective transparent plastic shields, but she had reached a point in the experiment where she needed to get at the apparatus. So she raised one shield and pulled the other aside.

As she did, the materials exploded, blowing glass and searing chemicals into her face, shoulders, and arms. In an instant, Dudak was aflame.

The heat was so intense that her safety goggles melted into her hair. She was certain that she was going to die, and as she slipped into unconsciousness, she said to herself, "Dear God, here I come, ready or not."

At that point, Butler materialized in the doorway. He and Dudak were alone in the inferno, exactly as in the dream; two of Dudak's co-workers were on a coffee break, and one had fled in terror immediately after the explosion. Butler remembers groping through the fire, yelling out Dudak's name. When he found her, she looked just as she did in the dream. "She was burning like a wick," he recalls, "she was completely in flames, her whole body." Butler froze for a moment. Then, he says, "I guess I started acting like an automaton because I was playing out the dream. I was able to grab her leg, dragged her out of the flames and pulled her into my laboratory . . . and put her into this deluge shower."

Rita Dudak spent seven long months in the hospital. She and Butler, friends before the accident, have become extraordinarily close in the years since. "The spiritual bond is so strong," says Butler, "that we will be thinking about each other at the same time, she in Virginia, me in Pennsylvania, and we will telephone each other. It's just incredible."

Yet until his 1988 television appearance, Butler told no one except Dudak and those closest to him about his dream—the only one of its type he ever had. The scientist could not accept the existence of psychic phenomena. "I was almost ashamed that something mystical happened to me," he says. But he eventually came to terms with his experience. And although he is still the skeptical man of science, Butler now feels that on this one occasion, he was for some unknown reason shown the future and carefully instructed on how to deal with it. Courage had absolutely nothing to do with saving Rita Dudak's life, he insists. "It was not heroism," he said. "It was as though the dream had prepped me for this incident. I know that if I hadn't had the dream, I wouldn't have behaved as I did. People just don't walk into fires."

Remarkable though it was, Edward Butler's experience is not by any means unique. Just as everyone dreams, so numbers of people—perhaps thousands, perhaps many more—seem to have psychic dreams at some time or other in their lives. In one study of 290 random dream reports, researchers found to their amazement that, if the reports were true, 38 of them—8.8 percent—could be classified as paranormal to one extent or another. That is, they exhibited qualities that could not be explained by ordinary means.

Such dreams have probably occurred since the earliest days of humankind, although only in relatively modern times has there been a concerted effort to quantify and qualify the phenomenon. The dreamers are everybody—from the humblest laborer to the most renowned public figure. Many dreamers have been men of letters: Both Charles Dickens and Rudyard Kipling dreamed in detail of events that subsequently occurred, while H. Rider Haggard visualized the agonizing demise of a faithful pet retriever and Mark Twain sadly previewed the death of his beloved younger brother.

By their very nature, psychic dreams tend to be of con-

Dire Visions of Disaster

"On the April night of the *Titanic* disaster, when I was five," wrote novelist Graham Greene in his autobiography, *A Sort of Life,* "I dreamt of a shipwreck. One image of the dream has remained with me for more than sixty years: a man in oilskins bent double beside a companion-way under the blow of a great wave." More than a week earlier, London businessman J. Connon Middleton—who had booked passage on the luxury ocean liner but later postponed his trip—had also dreamed of the catastrophe, but in far grimmer detail.

Middleton dreamed two nights in a row that the ship was sinking while people struggled around it. At least nineteen other cases of precognition through dreams, trances, and visions have been associated with that fateful night of April 14, 1912, when the *Titanic* struck an iceberg and over 1,500 people drowned.

Because disaster is a common dream theme, skeptics dismiss the examples above as coincidence. Others, however, think that the more calamitous an event, the more likely it is that people will pick

it up through dreams or visions. For example, researchers have recorded two dozen supposedly premonitory dreams related to the tragic 1966 coal-waste avalanche in Aberfan, Wales, in which 116 children and 28 adults died. People all over Britain reported nightmares of being enveloped in blackness or of their rooms caving in. A little girl from the village itself dreamed that something black had covered her school. One day later, she lay dead beneath the huge wave of black rubble that crushed the building.

Survivors of the Titanic—whose last message appears below—await rescue in the photo at left. A woman who escaped onto an overloaded lifeboat recalled concentrating on her daughter during the ordeal. Reportedly at the same time, the daughter—in New York and unaware that her mother was on a ship—dreamed that her mother was in a lifeboat that was in great danger of capsizing.

sequence. Yet the annals of dream research are filled with such diverse and trifling episodes as a premonition about a fishing rod, foreknowledge of a visit from strangers, or the vision of a woman wearing a red dress—all of them as difficult to explain as dreams that foretold much more important events. The dreams themselves include not only precognitive, or future-telling, dreams but clairvoyant and telepathic dreams that see the unseen and communicate the unknown, concurrent and reciprocal dreams that involve two or more dreamers, and dreams that transmit messages from the dead.

Skeptics hold that so-called psychic dreams can easily be explained away. In the first place, the validity of most accounts of dreams that tell the future depends entirely on the word of the person who claimed to have the dream. Only occasionally has a dream been related to another individual before the supposedly confirming event takes place, and then the verifying party is usually someone with a close personal relationship to the dreamer, say a spouse. It is rare indeed to find a record of a precognitive dream that was described to independent witnesses before rather than after the event it predicted came to pass.

Another obvious explanation is simple coincidence; a person dreams of a yellow car going the wrong way on a one-way street and, sure enough, just happens to witness such a scene shortly thereafter. A more sophisticated counterargument to psychic dreams suggests that the unconscious holds a great deal more knowledge and is considerably more perceptive than is generally supposed. This line of reasoning says the unconscious picks up real but not

An Explosive Premonition

While stationed in South Africa in the spring of 1902, a British soldier named John William Dunne dreamed he was on an island in imminent peril from a volcano—or so Dunne wrote later. "Forthwith," he recounted, "I was seized with a frantic desire to save the 4,000 (I knew the number) unsuspecting inhabitants." For the rest of the nightmare, he tried to persuade the "incredulous French authorities" to remove the islanders to safety.

Some time after Dunne's disturbing dream, a newspaper delivered to his camp featured the story of the devastating eruption of Mount Pelée on the French island of Martinique in the West Indies. Much of the information, the astonished Dunne noted, including the number of lives lost, coincided with his dream. (In fact, he had misread the account, which estimated 40,000, not 4,000, deaths—a mistake he did not discover until fifteen years later.)

Dunne said that other dreams presaging disaster followed in the next few years, leading him to conclude that something more than coincidence was involved. Still, he believed his visions were not occult prophecies but were instead previews of his own personal experiences. For instance, instead of foreseeing a disaster, he anticipated his reading about it in the newspaper. Somehow, he thought, dreams mixed one's images of the future with those of the past—a theory he later elaborated in his 1927 book, *An Experiment with Time.*

consciously noticed clues, assesses them against a framework of information that is not consciously remembered, and deduces a likely development that is later emitted in the form of a dream. It is this mundane mental operation, the skeptics say, not some mysterious psi, that accounts for "psychic" dreams.

"It is true," agrees psychologist Gayle Delaney, "that many so-called psychic dreams are no more than lucky guesses or logical projections into the future." And it is likewise true, she continues, that "the dreamer's subconscious, having had access to consciously forgotten memories and subtle, unrecognized perceptions, is capable of producing dreams that can seem psychic but that, in fact, are not." Yet Delaney and other researchers insist that hard evidence developed by rigorous research indicates that psychic dreams do occur. Says psychologist H. J. Eysenck of the University of London, "Unless there is a gigantic conspiracy involving some thirty university departments all over the world and several hundred highly respected scientists . . . the only conclusion the unbiased observer can come to must be that there does exist a small number of people who obtain knowledge existing in other people's minds or in the outer world by means as yet unknown to science."

By far the most commonly recorded psychic dream is the one that casts into the future, sometimes looking ahead only a few hours or days, sometimes years. Often such precognitive dreams picture dire circumstances. But that is not always the case, as the townspeople of Swaffham, in Norfolk, England, will happily attest. They cherish the legendary account of a splendid dream, one that visited a fifteenth-century ancestor and devoted churchgoer named John Chapman. Indeed, in their church of Saints Peter and Paul, they have raised statues to Mr. Chapman, to his wife, to his children, and even to his dog.

A humble peddler, Chapman one night had a dream in which he was instructed to go to London where a man on London Bridge would inform him of a great treasure that was to be his. Too poor to travel by horse or cart, Chapman tramped ninety miles to London and for three days waited on the bridge. At last a curious shopkeeper came out to inquire of his business, and Chapman related his dream but in embarrassment did not reveal his name or that of his town.

"I am sorry for thee, my good friend," responded the shopkeeper. "Now if I heeded dreams I might have proved myself as very a fool as thou hast; for it is not long since that I dreamt that at a place called Swaffham Market, in Norfolk, dwells one John Chapman, a pedlar. He hath a tree in his back garden, so I dreamed, under which is buried a pot of money. Now suppose I journeyed all the way thither because of that dream in order to dig for that money, what a fool I should be!"

Chapman, no fool, had his message and hurried home to dig under his old pear tree. There, he uncovered a pot full of gold and silver coins. And on the lid of the grimy pot was an inscription: "Under me doth lye / Another much richer than I." Digging down farther, Chapman found a chest with an even greater treasure, which he cannily concealed from his neighbors until the day came when the town decided to refurbish their church. When the people met to levy the tax to pay for the construction, Chapman asked how much it would cost. When they told him, he smilingly announced that he would pay for the entire thing and for a tall new steeple as well. Then, for the first time, the citizens of Swaffham were told what had come to John Chapman in a dream.

Apocryphal as it may sound, this tale meets all the criteria for a precognitive dream. And it remains a fact that one John Chapman, a simple artisan, did donate funds for the renovation of Swaffham's fine church.

Among the most interesting facets of Chapman's dream and the dream of the London shopkeeper is that they gave specific details about real places. Numerous cases have been just as precise, though perhaps not as rewarding. At the turn of the century, for example, a popular Victorian novelist named William Howitt reported an amazingly detailed prevision of his brother's home near Melbourne, Australia. Howitt experienced the dream on shipboard while

A clairvoyant dream proved the undoing of nineteenth-century murderer William Corder (left). In 1827, Maria Marten of Suffolk, England, eloped with Corder, a farmer. After several months, the girl's parents began to wonder why they had not heard from her. Then Maria's mother dreamed three nights in a row that her daughter had been killed and buried in a red barn. The distraught woman convinced the authorities to pull up the floor of Corder's barn, and there they found the girl's corpse. The farmer was tried and hanged for the murder, depicted in the contemporary illustration below.

traveling to his brother's new abode for the first time. The brother had not described the place, yet Howitt said that every aspect of the establishment—the house and the brick outbuildings, the hill on which they stood, the nearby eucalyptus forest—came to him with clarity and accuracy. He was astonished when he arrived and discovered how exactly the actual place matched his dream.

Yet most precognitive dreams involve people and events, and most of those visions are prophecies of woe. Among the more intriguing cases in recent years was one that involved a housewife, Mrs. Barbara Garwell, of Hull, England. Modestly educated, the mother of four children, a pleasant and apparently stable personality, Garwell scarcely seems the psychic sort, although she is superstitious about a number of things.

Nonetheless, in early March 1981, Garwell had a vivid dream in which she was riding in a car with two Germans wearing the black uniforms of Adolf Hitler's elite force, the SS. A large limousine was approaching. It stopped, and out of it stepped a man with a pockmarked face, whom Garwell, on waking, uncertainly identified as the actor Trevor Howard. The two SS men got out of their car. One of them drew a pistol and fired several shots at the actor, who fell to the ground. Three weeks later, on March 30, 1981, Ronald Reagan, president of the United States and a one-time movie star, was stepping out of his limousine in Washington, D.C., when John W. Hinckley, Jr., shot and severely wounded him. Hinckley had become a member of a neo-Nazi group in 1978, but he had been expelled because his ideas were too violent and extreme.

Relating Garwell's dream to the assassination attempt requires a long reach for connections (Hinckley's obscure neo-Nazi tie, for instance), some fairly convoluted interpretation (actor Trevor Howard as a stand-in for President Reagan), overlooking inaccuracies (two assailants instead of one), and ignoring the likely effect on the dreamer of the pervasive, continual presence of news and movies about assassinations and other acts of violence. If it were Garwell's only alleged precognitive dream, it probably would

have been dismissed with a laugh. But it was not.

In September of that same year, she experienced a vivid dream in which she saw a sort of "stadium" holding a single row of seated men, all with "coffee-colored skins" and wearing dark suits. The locale was somewhere in the Middle East, she knew, with "sand nearby." To her horror, Garwell saw two soldiers, also "coffee-colored," rush up to the row of men and spray them with automatic-rifle fire. Three weeks later, on October 6, 1981, President Anwar Sadat of Egypt was assassinated during a parade. As an armored unit passed in review, four disaffected Egyptian soldiers jumped down and ran to the grandstand, one hurling hand grenades and the others spraying the helpless dignitaries with bursts of fire from assault rifles. Sadat was wearing a dark blue uniform.

The year was almost out when Garwell had yet another dream. In it, she observed a ship at sea. Two coffins descended slowly from the ship, sliding down a sort of "rope gang-way," as she called it. Garwell believed the ship to be the one on which two of her friends were booked for a cruise to South Africa—the Italian liner *Achille Lauro*. She did not tell her two friends; she had no desire to alarm them, and the deaths did not seem to be associated with them. Three weeks later, on December 2, 1981, fire broke out on the *Achille Lauro*, 100 miles off the Canary Islands. Garwell's friends were uninjured, but in all the smoke and confusion, two other passengers died of heart attacks.

Later, when dream researchers asked Garwell if she could think of anything that might have laid the foundation for her apparent psychic abilities, she recalled that three times as a child she had fallen and hit her head in the same spot and that she had required stitches each time.

A knock on the head or no, some psychical investigators place considerable faith in Garwell's dreams. In each case, she described her precognition to others well before the events, and those witnesses signed statements to that effect. Her details were far from perfect, but they did broadly suggest many elements of the real events and were fairly

precise in others. Moreover, in the view of researchers, the consistent time period between dream and fulfillment in itself seemed to enhance the acceptability of the report.

There was very little that Garwell could do about her premonitions, of course, but in a number of other cases, psychic dreamers apparently have been able to affect actual events. Atlanta psychotherapist David Ryback reports the case of a young man who dreamed that he was speeding along a road at night and hit the brakes as he entered a curve; his car skidded, went off the road, and was heavily damaged. Some nights later, he was driving along that same road at a pretty fair clip and came to the curve. As he approached, he remembered the dream and slowed his speed, not needing to brake. He saw a dark stain on the road and, curious about it, stopped to investigate. The stain turned out to be an oil slick. "If I had put on my brakes right there before the curve," the young man wrote Ryback, "I surely would have skidded off the road."

Ryback describes another example, involving a family in which a woman and her son, sister, and nephew all experienced psychic dreams. The sister, named Ella, had a particularly vivid dream of disaster that she believes she averted by altering her actions. In the dream, Ella was on a camping trip and went down to the riverbank with her four-year-old son to wash out some clothes. Then she realized that she had forgotten the soap. As she walked back to get it, Ella saw, out of the corner of her eye, her young son fling a stone into the water, lose his balance, and tumble in. She rushed to him, but the current swept him away and he drowned. "She awoke very upset," writes Ryback.

On the family's next outing, the woman and her son went down to the river with some dirty clothes—and she discovered that she had no soap. As she turned back, she glimpsed her son raise his arm to loft a rock into the river. Instantly, Ella spun around and grabbed the lad just as he was teetering into the water, giving him, says Ryback, "a long, long hug." Continues the doctor: "These dream experiences suggest that although the future may be written, the script can be revised. Or part of the future is written and the rest depends on the dreamer's response."

Yet sometimes there is no reason for any response other than scratching one's head in amazement. Consider the dream a housewife described in a letter to psychoanalyst and dream therapist Montague Ullman. In her sleep the woman had seen her younger sister standing before her wearing a bulky coat. The sister's hands were in the coat pockets. When she pulled them out, they were filled with bottle caps. That was it, the whole dream. The following noon, the sister, her husband, and two sons arrived for Father's Day dinner. The sister, who was pregnant, had on a full, lightweight summer coat. She reached in the pockets and pulled out two big handfuls of bottle caps, exclaiming delightedly, "Look at what the boys put in my pockets."

If the precognitive dream is a psychic look into the future, the supposed clairvoyant dream focuses more or less on the moment. The dreamer visualizes distant scenes and events, sees and recognizes people, listens to their conversations, and observes their actions—later to discover in astonishment that it all took place exactly as dreamed and often at exactly the same instant.

These visions are frequently of great peril or death, often befalling a loved one. It is easy to understand, then, why some believers think the force of the emotion involved in the actual event somehow impresses itself on the dreamer's unconscious. They suggest such a mechanism might have been at work in 1912, when a young woman said she saw her mother in a lifeboat rocking on an ocean swell, "a lifeboat," the daughter related, "so crowded with people that it looked as if it might be swamped at any minute." The woman later learned that her mother had been on the ill-fated *Titanic* and was at the time of the dream in a jam-packed lifeboat that was wallowing on a dark sea, never expecting to see her daughter again.

But sometimes the dream picture appears devoid of powerful emotion or holds no people whatsoever, merely inanimate objects. The dream may even seem utterly trivial yet nonetheless appears inexplicable by conventional standards. William Oliver Stevens, an educator and author on psychic research, believed that such petty, clairvoyant dreams are far more commonplace than supposed.

He cited three examples. The mother of the Portuguese ambassador under President James Buchanan dreamed that her son was at a dinner party in muddy boots and, in embarrassment, kept his feet hidden under the table; in fact, his carriage had met with an accident resulting in his boots being muddied. A woman dreamed that she received a note on blue paper fashioned into a three-cornered fold, containing the rules for a game called Kriegspiel and signed by a certain name; she subsequently found an identical note, which she was sure she had never seen before in real life, on her piano. And an executive dreamed of a damp order sheet covered with smeared, illegible writing; some time later, precisely such a sheet arrived at his office. "Taken separately, these trivial but true dreams seldom make more than little scraps of stories," says Stevens, "but a whole collection of them becomes impressive."

However, certain clairvoyant dreams of inanimate—or at least lifeless—objects have been seen to have great substance. A classic example dates back to 1898 and was in fact among the first investigations conducted by Professor William James, the Harvard psychologist who became a fa-

Like terrifying images from a nightmare, this series of photographs captures successive moments in the brutal assassination of Egyptian president Anwar Sadat on October 6, 1981. Machine-gun wielding soldiers leaped from a truck in the parade, ran toward the grandstand, and sprayed its occupants with automatic gunfire. Three weeks before the actual incident, Barbara Garwell of Hull, England, allegedly dreamed a strikingly similar scene of a bloody assassination set in the Middle East.

Preview of a Hanging

In England in 1774, while waiting for their friend, poet Anna Seward, to join them, a Mr. Cunningham reportedly told his companion Mr. Newton about two vivid dreams he had had the night before. In the first, he heard a horse and rider approaching. As Cunningham watched, three men jumped out of a thicket, stopped the horse, searched the rider's clothes and boots, and then took him prisoner. At this point, Cunningham related, he awoke. By and by, he fell asleep again and was soon back in a dream. This time he was standing with a crowd in front of a gallows, where a man was being hanged—the very man, in fact, who had been arrested in his first dream.

Shortly thereafter Miss Seward arrived with a young protégé, John André, a newly commissioned British officer who was shortly to join his regiment in Canada. According to the story, Cunningham stared at the young man as if he were a ghost. He later explained his strange behavior to Newton: André, he stated, was the very man he had seen in his dreams.

Six years later, the two friends had cause to remember that dream, when news reached them that the Americans had executed Major John André as a spy. He had been convicted of conspiring with Benedict Arnold to overthrow the American fortress of West Point. Moreover, the details of his capture and death coincided with Cunningham's alleged dream. André was caught by three militiamen, who searched his clothes and boots, where they found incriminating documents. And he was hanged *(right)*, as the dream had previewed.

If true as told, this story merits interest not only as an example of precognitive dreaming but because six years elapsed between dream and fulfillment—a long time compared with other reports of dreams that supposedly have predicted the future.

mous philosopher and helped found the American Society for Psychical Research. As James reported in the proceedings of the ASPR, on October 31 of that year, a young woman named Bertha Huse had vanished in Enfield, Vermont, and no amount of searching turned up a trace of her. The only clue came from the blacksmith's wife, who recalled seeing a woman resembling Bertha on Shaker Bridge at the north end of Muscova Lake.

On the morning of the disappearance, a Mrs. Nellie Titus, living four-and-a-half miles distant, awoke to tell her husband that something terrible had happened. He shrugged and went off to work. By evening, everyone in the area, including Mrs. Titus, had heard about Bertha Huse, and they knew that a professional diver had been called in to search beneath the bridge, but to no avail.

After supper that evening, Mrs. Titus sat dozing in her chair. When her husband roused her, she came to with a start, asking him crossly, "Why didn't you let me be? In the morning I could have told you where the girl lays and all about it." That night in bed, her husband heard her mutter, "She's not down there, but over here on the left." Again he awakened her, and she begged him to leave her be.

The next night, Mrs. Titus awoke, said that she knew where the girl was, and insisted that her husband accompany her there in the morning. Shortly after 8:00 a.m., Mrs. Titus and her husband arrived at the Shaker Bridge. She walked to a particular spot, pointed, and said, "She's down there."

The diver was called back to the scene, protesting that he had searched the area thoroughly. "No," said Mrs. Titus, gesturing in exasperation. "You have been there and there, but not there. She is head down in the mud, one foot sticking up and a new rubber on it." The diver submerged again, and when he surfaced, he was shaken. Bertha Huse's body lay eighteen feet down, head first in the mud, with one leg up and a new rubber shoe on one foot. "It is my business to recover bodies in the water, and I am not afraid of them," said the diver. "But in this instance I was afraid of the woman on the bridge."

Professor James was able to establish that Mrs. Titus had experienced other clairvoyant dreams but had fought against "the power," as she called it, because it always left her ill. He concluded that the report was a "decidedly solid document in favor of the admission of a supernormal faculty of seership."

At about the time that James was investigating Nellie Titus's clairvoyant dream, other psychical researchers were commencing their study of a somewhat less common but closely related sleep phenomenon. This was the telepathic dream, in which thoughts, emotions, even physical sensations seem to be transmitted intentionally from one mind to another, sometimes across great distances.

The exciting thing about such dreams is that they are the most susceptible of all forms to scientific inquiry. Since a precognitive or clairvoyant dream seems to depend primarily on the perceptions of the dreamer, researchers must content themselves with checking facts and veracity. But a telepathic dream actively involves both a transmitter and a receiver; thus, experiments can be set up in an attempt to duplicate and analyze the phenomenon.

Among the first to experiment with telepathic dreaming at the turn of the century was an Italian psychical researcher named G. B. Ermacora. Like every educated Italian, he had grown up hearing the story of how in 1321 the lost cantos of Dante's *Divine Comedy* had been recovered through a telepathic dream. According to Dante's contemporary Giovanni Boccaccio, who wrote of it in his celebrated tales of Flo-

A Dream of Assassins

Monsignor de Lanyi, bishop of Grosswardin in Hungary, reportedly awoke with a start from an alarming nightmare in the early morning hours of June 28, 1914. The bishop, who had once tutored the Austrian archduke Franz Ferdinand in Hungarian, dreamed that he went to his writing table and found a black-bordered letter addressed to him in the hand of his former pupil. He opened the letter and saw at its head a picture rather like a postcard, with a crowded street and a short alley on it. The archduke and his wife were shown sitting in an automobile with three men. Suddenly, the picture seemed to come to life, as two young men sprang from the crowd and shot the royal couple with revolvers. The words underneath the scene supposedly read, "Dear Dr. Lanyi, I herewith inform you that today my wife and I will fall victims to an assassination. We commend ourselves to your pious prayers." It was signed by the archduke.

Later that morning the bishop allegedly told his mother and a houseguest of his dream and then said a mass for the archduke and his wife. That afternoon he received a cable that confirmed his dreadful vision. Franz Ferdinand and his wife were murdered that very day while on a state visit to Serbia *(below)*, and the circumstances closely resembled Lanyi's dream.

The only difference, Lanyi said, was that he saw two assassins, when there had in fact been just one. But Lanyi apparently did not write down the details of his dream until two years had passed, and no witnesses are on record corroborating that he told people about it before he learned of the actual assassination. Thus the validity of his claim to having dreamed in advance the event that precipitated World War I depends entirely on trusting the bishop as a man of his word.

English actress Mrs. Patrick Campbell (left), better known as Mrs. Pat, reportedly made her last appearance not on a stage, but in a friend's dream. Living in Hollywood in 1940, actress Sara Allgood dreamed that her friend Mrs. Pat alighted from a train car and uttered with her trademark air of boredom, "Have you found my gift from the grave? Look behind the picture." The next morning Allgood took down a watercolor Mrs. Pat had given her years earlier. Behind the backing was a Max Beerbohm caricature of the actress, reckoned to be worth more than 1,000 dollars. A few days later, Sara read of Mrs. Pat's death in France.

rentine life, Dante had died just as he was concluding his epic poem, and the final cantos were discovered to be missing.

Dante's son Jacopo, a sometime poet himself, was urged to complete the work—a "presumptuous folly," thought Boccaccio—but before he could start, his father appeared to him in a dream. Dante, wrote Boccaccio, was "clothed in the purest white, and his face resplendent with an extraordinary light; Jacopo asked him if he lived, and Dante replied: 'Yes, but in the true life, not our life.'" Then Jacopo asked his father if he had finished his work, and if so, what had happened to it. Dante confirmed that he had completed it and then "took him, Jacopo, by the hand and led him into that chamber in which he, Dante, had been accustomed to sleep when he lived in this life: and, touching one of the walls, he said: 'What you have sought for so much is here'; and at these words, both Dante and sleep fled from Jacopo at once."

Returning to Dante's house the next day, Jacopo and a friend located what Boccaccio called "a little window in the wall, never before seen by any of them. . . . In it they found several writings, all mouldy from the dampness of the walls, and had they remained there longer, in a little while they would have crumbled away. They found them to be the 13 cantos that had been wanting to complete the Commedia."

Ermacora was inclined to believe the tale, but he could not explain it. Then as luck would decree it, a medium named Maria Manzini told

him of a curious occurrence. It seemed that Maria's four-year-old cousin Angelina was staying with her and that the child had awakened one morning to describe a dream about a little girl named Elvira. This astonished Maria; Elvira was her own secret spirit control, or trance personality. What was more, Elvira had promised to appear in Angelina's dreams again that night, this time wearing a pink dress and carrying a beautiful doll.

The next day, Maria informed Ermacora that the visit had taken place in Angelina's dreams, almost precisely as Elvira had said it would. Excitedly, the researcher decided to try a series of experiments with the Manzinis. On fifty-nine occasions, he gave Maria sets of clues, which presumably she would absorb into her own consciousness. Ermacora's idea was that if the clues subsequently turned up in the child's dreamscape, the only explanation was that they had been implanted telepathically by Maria's spirit guide while the child was sleeping. Evidently, the scheme worked to his satisfaction, because Ermacora pronounced the results of

In 1904, English novelist H. Rider Haggard dreamed he saw his daughter's black retriever lying among brushwood by water. The dog, he wrote, "transmitted to my mind in an undefined fashion the knowledge that it was dying." After waking, he described the dream to his wife. The next day the dog was missing, and Haggard embarked on a search. He found its body floating against a weir about a mile from home. The novelist concluded that the animal had communicated with him by "placing whatever portion of my being is capable of receiving such impulses when enchained by sleep, into its own terrible position."

his studies highly promising and cited numerous examples of telepathic material that had been induced in Angelina's dream consciousness.

Although Ermacora's experiments mark the first serious attempts at inducing dream telepathy with a preselected sender and receiver, his methods seem ludicrous by modern standards. A large proportion of the evidence was gathered by Maria and related to him secondhand several hours later. The possibility that Maria, who made her living as a professional medium, might be tempted to shape the reports of a four-year-old in such a way as to prolong the

investigation seems not to have occurred to the doctor.

Ermacora's experiments received only passing notice, and research in dream telepathy was largely ignored for several decades. Then, in the 1940s, Wilfrid Daim, a young Viennese psychologist, rekindled scientific curiosity with the first truly workable method for studying dream telepathy in a controlled setting. Daim segregated senders and receivers—sometimes positioning them in distant areas of the same building, sometimes miles apart. Then he gave the senders an image that neither they nor their receivers could possibly know about beforehand and asked them to trans-

mit it telepathically to the sleeping receivers. Next the psychologist recorded the dream content of the receivers verbatim before they had a chance to become contaminated by outside influences. In one typical experiment, conducted at 6:30 a.m. on March 14, 1948, and set forth later in Duke University's *Parapsychological Bulletin*, Daim took the part of the sender. Sitting in a closed room at a considerable distance from the sleeping receiver, he chose at random from a collection of envelopes on the table and found as his "target" image a red equilateral triangle on a black background. He began to concentrate on the image, hoping to project his thoughts across space to his receiver. He wrote that he felt a "strange telepathic contact which is nearly impossible to describe. Then I energetically ordered the awakening of the receiver but not with words."

Down the hall, Daim's receiver awoke at 6:35 a.m. He recalled a dream in which there were mounted soldiers, music, and much excitement, into which "suddenly a three-cornered, glaring-red fir tree pushes through the whole . . . and remains unmoved for seconds amid all the former dream contents. It is not a fir tree out of nature but such a one as one finds in children's primers." In other words, his dream was interrupted by an image that seemed very like the one that Daim was targeting in his consciousness. And it had come to the dreamer at a moment virtually synchronous with Daim's order to awaken.

As Daim was working alone in Austria a number of New York psychoanalysts began discussing their own views of telepathic dreaming. The group was well aware that people undergoing psychoanalysis often dreamed about their therapists. But what puzzled them were the many instances in which a patient's dreams were found to contain inexplicable information about the analyst's private life. Was this, they asked, some form of genuine psychic interaction?

One member of the group, Montague Ullman, who was already known for his role in therapeutic "dream work" and the "vigilance theory," in which he speculated that the alert dreaming brain stood watch while the body slept, decided to pursue the matter. Ullman knew the phenomenon of psychic dreaming from both sides of the couch. He himself had had several such dreams as a student-patient undergoing analysis, and later he had listened to patients describe dreams in which events from his own thoughts and life experiences were inexplicably embedded.

Ullman went on to examine the phenomenon of telepathic dreaming outside the patient-therapist environment.

He went looking for funding, and in 1962, with the help of Gardner Murphy, then vice-president of the ASPR and research director for the Menninger Foundation, an organization devoted to psychiatric research, he was ready to begin. Since Ullman was already the director of the Community Mental Health Center at Maimonides Medical Center in Brooklyn, New York, Maimonides became the site of the new dream laboratory. Working with Ullman were psychologist Stanley Krippner, four research assistants, and a number of volunteer subjects chosen for their ability to recall dreams and their generally favorable attitude toward ESP.

Over the next decade, the group ran several series of experiments, following essentially the same procedures and gradually refining their methods of evaluation. Typically, one of the subjects would arrive at the lab late at night, ready to go to sleep. He or she would enter the sleep room, be wired up with electrodes connected to a remote electroencephalograph monitor, and given instructions on the night's proceedings. In particular, the subject would be told to focus on identifying the target to be presented during sleep. He or she would then retire on the bed provided.

Meanwhile, in a second room, one of the staff, acting as the "experimenter," sat watching the EEG; and in a third room, soundproof except for a buzzer connected to the experimenter, another colleague (a "sender," or agent) waited for the signal to begin. When EEG activity indicated that the subject was entering his or her first REM, or dreaming, stage of sleep, the experimenter pushed the buzzer button that alerted the sender. The sender then opened a sealed envelope to discover the night's target picture, which usually came from a pool of twelve images.

The target pictures were reproductions of paintings by well-known artists. All the paintings were characterized by

In their 1973 book entitled Dream Telepathy, dream researchers Montague Ullman (left) and Stanley Krippner (below) wrote about their pioneering studies at the Maimonides Medical Center. "Perhaps our most basic finding," they concluded, "is the scientific demonstration of Freud's statement: 'Sleep creates favorable conditions for telepathy.'" The researchers observed that if a subject's dream "is vivid, colored, . . . and somewhat puzzling to the dreamer and does not 'fit' into his dream pattern or reflect recent activity, then we can be alerted to the possibility that the dream is being influenced by ESP."

strong emotional content—archetypal themes, vivid colors—elements that characterize the majority of reported spontaneous paranormal dreams and that presumably would make a powerful telepathic signal—if such signals exist. The sender was directed to concentrate on the target and attempt to mentally project that picture in any way he or she saw fit, including making mental images and writing down associative words.

When the EEG indicated that the REM period had ended, the sender was instructed to stop sending and the subject was awakened by the experimenter via an intercom. The subject was then asked to recount his or her dream into a tape recorder before returning to sleep. This same cycle of sleeping, dreaming, and post-dream debriefing was repeated as many as four or five times a night. The next morning, the session would conclude with the subject reviewing the night's dreams and adding any new associations that came to mind. The subject's full set of remarks were then transcribed and, together with copies of all of the illustrations in the target pool, were sent to three independent judges. Given no clues as to the actual target picture used by the agent, the judges were asked to rank the transcripts for correspondence with each of the targets. A target image deemed to have the most correct identifications was given a one, that with the fewest match-ups a twelve, and the remainder at various rankings in between.

Many of the early experiments produced inconclusive statistical results, but there were enough "hits" to convince Ullman and Krippner that they were on the right track. When, for example, research assistant Sally Van Steenburgh, as sender, concentrated on the image of George Bellows's *Dempsey and Firpo,* a darkly powerful painting of two prizefighters battling in New York's Madison Square Garden, her subject reported a dream involving "something about Madison Square Garden and a boxing fight." When she targeted *Mystic Night,* a painting by Millard Sheets depicting the dance ritual of five women in a verdant grove, her subject awoke to remember "being with a group of people . . . participating in something," and "a lot of mountains and trees." "What strikes me most about the whole thing was the trees, again, and the greenery and the country." The subject recalled "some sort of primitive aspect. . . . I can almost see it as some sort of tribal ritual in a jungle."

When research assistant Sol Feldstein projected *Zapatistas,* a painting by José Clemente Orozco portraying a band of Mexican-Indian followers of Zapata as they made their way across the mountains, the subject, a young psychologist named William Erwin, saw "traveling . . . a very distant scene" with "an aspect of grandeur about it." And he claimed to have had "a feeling of" New Mexico, seeing Indians and "a lot of mountains."

Ullman and Krippner felt that their dream laboratory had achieved its primary goal, which was to show not only that paranormal dreams could be rigorously studied but that they could be controlled to some degree. Now it was time to refine procedures. First, they analyzed the relative successes of subjects and agents in communicating with

each other. Erwin, the dreamer in the *Zapatistas* experiment, was singled out as the most responsive subject, Feldstein the most effective agent. The fact that Feldstein produced almost twice as many hits as the other agents also suggested that the agent was more than a passive participant, and this indicated that telepathy (ESP of the agent's thoughts), rather than clairvoyance (ESP of the target picture itself), was central to the process.

Feldstein's gifts were so pronounced that he even transmitted nontargeted material spontaneously from time to time. In one session the subject incorporated into a dream extraneous images that were seemingly scavenged from a textbook Feldstein was reading for his classwork, and on another night, when research assistant Joyce Plosky was the agent and Feldstein the EEG monitor, his telepathic signal was so strong that it apparently "jammed" hers; none of Plosky's transmission reached the subject's dream consciousness, but something on Feldstein's mind did.

Ullman and Krippner decided to focus their next series of experiments on the dream telepathy potential of Erwin as subject and Feldstein as agent, and in the fall of 1964, they ran the two men through seven nights of dream induction experiments. This time the results were even more dramatic than in previous rounds. The three judges who reviewed the transcripts found that five out of the seven transmissions had been hits. In one example, the night Feldstein's target picture was Degas's *School of the Dance,* Erwin was given a nearly perfect score, for dreaming about being "in a class" in which "at different times, different people would get up for some sort of recitation or some sort of contribution. . . . There was one little girl that was trying to dance with me."

Still, skeptics were not convinced; they argued that almost any dream could be found to have some correspondence with almost any target if one were disposed to look for it. In response, Ullman and Krippner made the judging process even more sophisticated and the sending-receiving effort more varied in its appeal to the dreamer. Feldstein received an assortment of physical props by which he could reinforce projection of his target picture, rather as a charade player would act out a secret password. To send an image of the target painting *Interior of the Synagogue,* for example, he was given candles to light and an object inscribed in Hebrew; to send Daumier's *The Barrel Organ,* which shows a group of people singing hymns around an organ, Feldstein received a hymnal. This time around, on six of the eight nights the correspondence between Erwin's dreams and the target pictures were found by the judges to be "direct hits," and the remaining two nights fell just short of "direct." By Ullman's calculations, the odds against so many pure coincidences occurring were 1,000 to 1.

The Maimonides team now wondered what kind of telepathic transference might take place when a large number of agents were mobilized to send a message to a dreaming receiver. After preliminary tests, they settled on a plan to work with audiences of the Grateful Dead, a popular rock group. They chose as the principal setting a concert hall in Port Chester, New York, where the band was to give six late-night performances in February 1971. Two apparently gifted psychic sensitives, Malcolm Bessent and Felicia Parise, were selected to be the simultaneous subjects. Bessent was to sleep at Maimonides under the usual experimental conditions; Parise, functioning as a control, was to sleep in her own apartment, awakening on cue every ninety minutes when the lab called for the latest dream report.

On the appointed nights, Bessent and Parise retired to their respective hideaways at 10:00 p.m. Around 11:30, when the two were asleep, the 2,000 fans at the concert hall forty-five miles away were given a brief description of what the dream laboratory was trying to do. Then the following instructions were flashed on a large screen that was located above the stage.

"You are about to participate in an ESP experiment. In a few seconds you will see a picture. Try using your ESP to 'send' this picture to Malcolm Bessent. He will try to dream about the picture. Try to 'send' it to him. Malcolm Bessent is now at the Maimonides dream laboratory in Brooklyn."

As part of the control, Parise's involvement was not mentioned at any time. If Parise and Bessent were equally successful in receiving telepathic impressions, it would suggest that telepathy works chiefly through the "reaching out" of the subject; if, however, there was a significant difference in the results, "intentionality" on the part of the agents, who were trying to contact Bessent but were unaware of Parise, would have to be reckoned as a significant factor.

While the band played, a randomly selected art print was projected before the audience, whose "states of consciousness" in the words of Stanley Krippner, were already "dramatically altered . . . by the music, by the ingestion of psychedelic drugs before the concert started, and by contact with other members of the audience." When the accumulated results of six nights' experiments were evaluated, the anonymous Parise's dreams scored no better than chance would explain. But Bessent scored very well four times out of six. On one night, for example, when fans were "sending" their versions of *The Seven Spinal Chakras,* an image of a man in lotus position with his chakras, or energy centers, all vividly colored, Bessent was dreaming about a man who was "suspended in mid-air or something" and "using natural energy." He remembered "the light from the sun . . . a spinal column." The Maimonides team concluded that ESP had to be the only explanation for Bessent's high number of correspondences, but they added with admirable caution, "This experiment does not prove that 2,000 agents are better than a single agent."

Bessent's psychic dreaming talents apparently were not limited to telepathy. For a study in precognitive dreaming, the Maimonides team again chose Bessent as their subject. The study lasted sixteen nights, with each experiment covering two nights: On the first night, Bessent would attempt to dream precognitively about a target picture that he would view the following night. On the second night, Bessent would see the target and then attempt to dream about it. The entire sequence began again on the third night, with a different target. At the end of the complete series, it was judged that on the eight precognitive-dreaming nights, Bessent scored seven hits; on the eight control nights, Bessent's dream images bore little or no resemblance to the target pictures. Again, the odds against this happening by chance were calculated at 1,000 to 1.

Despite such compelling study results, the Maimonides experiments came to an end in 1972 when research funds ran out and the principals moved on to other places and other tasks. Summarizing their work, Ullman and Krippner have concluded that people who are open to the possibility of ESP, who are relatively comfortable in the laboratory, and who are able to remember their dreams have a reasonable probability of experiencing psychic dreams in an experimental situation.

Such people have an even higher likelihood of psi retrieval if the pictures selected as targets contain emotionally powerful images with which the subject and agent can personally identify. Male participants generally scored higher than women on target material incorporating themes of sex and aggression, which the researchers explained by the fact that men in general are more inclined to dream about these themes. Similarly, as women in general tend to be more sensitive to the colors and linear details of images than men, so females in a laboratory setting gave more accurate reports of the colors and details of their art targets. Themes involving eating, drinking, religious subject matter—basic concerns of both sexes—tended to come through well with all participants in all combinations.

Unfortunately, no one has since come close to replicating the Maimonides experiments. Sleep researchers at the University of Wyoming in Laramie tried twice and failed. Cynics suggest that the Maimonides team fooled themselves into seeing paranormal connections because that was what they were hoping to find. Others feel that just as the positive atmosphere at Maimonides had given the experimenters' psi capability the best chance to find expression, so the latent hostility in Laramie had throttled it. David Foulkes, who supervised the Wyoming experiments, concedes that a highly skeptical attitude may have tainted his results. "It proved hard to es-cape the role of protector of scientific purity or guardian of the scientific morals," he says. "Were we sympathetic and encouraging observers, or scientific detectives out to prevent a crime from being committed before our very eyes?"

Such skepticism from the scientific community, along with the prohibitive costs of operating a dream laboratory, have forced researchers to explore the phenomenon from new perspectives—those that present psychic dreaming in a way that is, as one researcher put it, "more acceptable to contemporary science." Currently, much attention is being focused on the physiological functioning of the brain. And Maimonides alumnus Stanley Krippner, along with Michael A. Persinger, a professor of neuroscience and psychology at Laurentian University in Ontario, Canada, have undertaken an intriguing study using dream research collected from as far back as 1886 to examine the relationship between ESP and the earth's geomagnetic activity. Through such changes in direction and methodology, dream researchers hope to rekindle the interest of the scientific community in psychic dreaming and open the door for further studies.

Oblivious to all the scientific disarray over the subject are the nightly dreamers outside the laboratory walls, who keep right on experiencing what appear to be psychic dreams—and keep on wondering about them. Among the most complex and fascinating notions of psychic dreams are those labeled "reciprocal" and "concurrent." As defined by psi author William Oliver Stevens, concurrent means that two persons have identical or very similar dreams on the same night, whereas reciprocal means that the dreamers share a mutual experience—"that is," explains Stevens, "two or more people meet in their dreams on the same night and enact a scene together. Each is conscious of the other in the precise setting and action of the dream."

The dreams can be of real or imaginary events, trifling or heavy with meaning. An example of a dream that appears both concurrent and reciprocal comes from the *Proceedings of the Society for Psychical Research* in Britain. One night in August 1887, a Mrs. H dreamed that she was walking with her husband and a friend, Mr. J, in London's Richmond Park, when she saw a notice posted on a tree that a certain Lady R was giving a garden party at her country estate in honor of Queen Victoria's jubilee. Mrs. H's husband remarked that he hoped she would not go because it would be difficult to get back to town. At which point the friend said, "Oh, I will manage that for you," and Mrs. H woke up. Mrs. H's husband was awake as well and reported a vivid dream of his own. "I dreamt we were walking in Richmond Park," he said, "and I was told Lady R was going to have a party. We were invited, and I was very much troubled as to how we should get home, as the party was at ten and the last train went at eleven, when my friend J, who was walking with us, said, 'Oh, I will manage that for you.' " Unless Mr. and Mrs. H were a couple of Victorian pranksters—and apparently the SPR investigators did not think so—the case has to go down either as a coincidence in a million or as a striking example of paired psychic dreaming.

Reciprocal dreams are both rare and intricate. The London Dialectical Society published a report in 1873 about a Mr. Cromwell F. Varley visiting his sister-in-law, who was living in the country and critically ill with heart disease. On his first night in her home, Varley experienced a nightmare, in which he was totally paralyzed. As he lay there in his dream, he saw his sister-in-law enter the room and say to him, "If you do not move, you will die." But he could not move so much as a finger. Whereupon the sister-in-law said, "I will frighten you and then you will be able to move."

The sister-in-law made some attempts, but to no avail. By then, reported Varley, he was aware in the dream that his heart had stopped beating. At last, the sister-in-law screamed, "Oh, Cromwell, I am dying!" That terrified Varley. He jumped up, fully awake and with no trace of paralysis. By now, his wife was awake, and he told her about the apparition. They checked the door; it was bolted. They looked at the time; it was 3:45 a.m.

According to the report, Varley's sick sister-in-law complained the next morning of having passed a very bad night. She said that she dreamed of being in the Varleys' room and that Cromwell had been on the point of death. "I only succeeded in rousing you by exclaiming, 'Oh, Cromwell, I am dying!' " she said. "And at what time had the dream occurred?" Varley asked. "Between half-past three and four in the morning."

An even more elaborate reciprocal dream was supposedly reported to Robert Owen, a former member of the United States Congress and an emissary to Naples, Italy, in 1860. Once again, the dreaming involved two friends, one very ill, except in this instance the dreamers were hundreds of miles apart. The narrator was a Miss A.M.H., the daughter of a prominent literary figure in mid-Victorian England and a personal friend of Owen.

As related by Miss A.M.H., one night she dreamed that she journeyed to the town where her sick friend, S—, resided. She entered his house and went straight upstairs to a bed chamber. "There on his bed, I saw S— lying as if about to die," she recounted. "I took his hand and said, 'No, you are not going to die. Be comforted, you will live.' Even as I spoke I seemed to hear an exquisite strain of music sounding through the room."

Upon awakening, the young woman told her mother of the dream and then wrote S—, asking after his health but saying nothing about the dream. There the matter rested, until three years later, when she and her mother met their friend in London. The talk got around to dreams, and the lady told S— about her vision. A remarkable expression came over the gentleman's face, and he said that when he was so ill, shortly before her letter arrived, he had experienced a dream that was the very counterpart of hers.

In the dream, S— related, "I seemed to myself on the point of death," and asked his brother for two favors. "Send for my friend A.M.H. I must see her before I depart. I would also hear my favorite sonata by Beethoven ere I die." The brother protested: Did S— want nothing more than these trifles? But in his dream S— was adamant: "No. To see my friend A.M.H.—and to hear the sonata. That is all I wish."

"And even as I spoke in my dream," S— related, "I

Dream researcher Charles Honorton,
who devised and supervised many of the
Maimonides laboratory dream
experiments, concentrates on a reproduction of Zapatistas, a painting by Mexican artist José Orozco, in an
attempt to transmit the image to a
dreaming volunteer in another room.
Chosen for its simplicity, vivid
colors, and deep emotional content, the
picture was one of a collection of 1,024
such images gathered by Honorton and his
associates for use as dream targets.

saw you enter. You walked up to the bed with a cheerful air, and, while the music I longed for filled the room, you spoke to me encouragingly, saying I should not die."

Former congressman Owen firmly vouched for the honesty of Miss A.M.H. Whether the gentleman identified as S— was the sort who could resist seizing an easy opportunity to impress and possibly win a lady by declaring an intimate dream relationship with her was not noted.

On a somewhat more prosaic, but nonetheless intriguing, level is a recent reciprocal dream that involves not two, but three, people and includes elements of telepathy, clairvoyance, and precognition. A young woman named Wynona, living in central Florida, dreamed that her racecar-driver brother was working on his stock car. "I saw him disconnect a small narrow rod that had a strong curled-up spring on each end," she recalled. "After he had fixed or done whatever he was doing to the car, he forgot to rehook that rod and spring." In her dream, the sister then saw her brother climb into the car, crank it up, and start to test-drive it. "I started yelling," she remembered, "trying to make myself heard over the loud noise of the engine. I can remember yelling and yelling." And there the dream ended.

er brother telephoned early the next morning and said that something scary had happened the previous night. He dreamed that his sister was yelling but that he could not understand her. At that point, the brother's wife woke him up, saying that she had just seen the sister's face over their bed and that something awful was wrong. They both got out of bed to look through the house to see whether the sister had come in during the night, but they found nothing.

Wynona then told her brother about the dream. He had not been working on the car but said he would check it. "He called within the hour," related Wynona, and said that "the cable that connects the brake pedal was broken and that if he had test-driven the car in that condition, he would surely have been wrecked."

Some believers propose that one dream can kindle or trigger another, that the unconscious mind acts as a sort of broadcast station sending out images and sound waves to other sleepers' sensitive mental receptors. And some theorize that a sort of psychic radar may operate in dreams, scanning for oncoming hostile blips and vectoring the unconscious on a course to defend and cope.

Science has long known that the brain generates electrical impulses, and a number of eminent scientists have attempted to create a model of the brain that, for starters, would accommodate telepathy. Sir John Carew Eccles, winner of a 1963 Nobel Prize in physiology, submits that there exist modules, or ensembles of neurons, in the cerebral cortex, and that each module "has to some degree a collective life of its own, with as many as 10,000 neurons of diverse types and with a functional arrangement of feed-forward and feedback excitation and inhibition." Each module, he says further, "may be likened to a radio transmitter-receiver unit." Be that as it may, present-day science, with systems sensitive enough to capture the slightest electrical impulse from outer space, has not yet been able to detect the dream waves rolling across the oceans of the night.

Another idea involves what Stanford University neuroscientist Karl Pribram calls the "holographic model," wherein all thoughts, images, and acts exist as a series of complex patterns within the whole picture. Every mind has a piece of the puzzle, and just as a computer can re-create

an entire pattern from just a piece of it, so the mind, in a dream, can employ what information it already has in order to complete other parts of the picture.

The inspiration for the holographic model comes from psychiatrist Carl Jung's view of the collective unconscious, in which everyone has access to all human experience, past, present, and future. And this experience as revealed in dreams, Jung believed, could be highly beneficial to the human psyche. Unlike his colleague and one-time mentor Sigmund Freud, who felt dreams were often expressions of hostility and neuroses, Jung said that they were restorative.

Indeed, the dream's well-documented ability to engender benevolence and understanding in the dreamer, to help in difficult situations, and to aid in contending with life and accepting the ultimate experience of death are among its most profound attributes. A woman in Atlanta found quiet comfort in a dream about her parents, who had journeyed to France to visit the Louvre and other treasure houses as members of an Atlanta museum society. Nothing particular happened or was said in the dream. The daughter just remembers visualizing her parents and seeing how very happy they were; she saw them vividly, from the colors of their clothes to the tiny smile crinkles around their eyes and mouths. When she awoke and looked at the clock it was 6:05 a.m. At that moment, at Paris's Orly Airport, the char-tered jet on which her parents were returning to Atlanta crashed on takeoff, killing all 106 passengers. The dream had not predicted disaster; there was nothing at all in it about death. The daughter simply experienced an intense physical image of the parents she loved, and that tender leave-taking always remained a great solace to her.

All of these dream experiences, says psychiatrist Montague Ullman, suggest "that while asleep, we are not only able to scan backward in time and tap into our remote memory, but are also able to scan forward in time and across space to tap into information outside our own experience. Regardless of how seldom they occur, these manifestations cast a new light on the range of our psychic abilities. They persuade us to look at dreams as events occurring in a much larger and more complex frame than we are accustomed."

It was that larger framework that Carl Jung was considering when he wrote, "The dream is the small hidden door in the deepest and most intimate sanctum of the soul, which opens into the primeval cosmic night. . . . In dreams we pass into the deeper and more universal truth and more eternal man, who still stands in the dusk of original night in which he himself was still the whole and the whole was in him in bright undifferentiated pure nature, free from the shackles of the ego."

Speculating that some of the successes in their dream telepathy experiments may have been due to the sender's emotional involvement with the target picture, Maimonides researchers decided in 1966 to give sender Sol Feldstein props to reinforce the impact of the paintings. While projecting George Bellows's Both Members of This Club (right), Feldstein wore a leather boxing glove. Accompanying Max Beckmann's The Descent from the Cross (left) were a wood cross, a representation of Jesus, tacks, a red pen, and instructions for Sol Feldstein to "nail Christ to the Cross and color his wounds red." The technique resulted in a high yield of dream telepathy far exceeding the researchers' expectations.

ACKNOWLEDGMENTS

The editors wish to thank the following individuals and institutions for their valuable assistance in the preparation of this volume:

Milo Beach, Director, Arthur M. Sackler Gallery, Smithsonian Institution, Washington, D.C.; Professor Hans Bender, Institut für Grenzgebiete der Psychologie und Psychohygiene, Freiburg, West Germany; Charles Butler, Ecumenecon, Silver Spring, Md.; Guido Cantoni, Direzione Generale Opere Salesiane Don Bosco, Rome; Nicholas Clark-Lowes, Society for Psychical Research, London; Don Giuseppe Costa, Direzione Generale Opere Salesiane Don Bosco, Rome; George Czuczka, Washington, D.C.; Rita Dwyer, Association for the Study of Dreams, Vienna, Va.; Dr. Keith Hearne, Hull, England; Professor Michel Jouvet, Directeur du Département de Médecine Expérimentale Université Claude-Bernard, Lyons, France; Professor Johannes Mischo, Institut für Parapsychologie, University of Freiburg, West Germany; Eleanor O'Keeffe, Society for Psychical Research, London; Marie-Thérèse Pellenc, Département de Médecine Expérimentale Université Claude-Bernard, Lyons, France; Christian Stephan, Freiburg, West Germany; Ann Stevens, London; Dr. Rolf Streichardt, Institut für Grenzgebiete der Psychologie und Psychohygiene, Freiburg, West Germany; Dr. Robert Van de Castle, Department of Behavioral Medicine and Psychiatry, University of Virginia Health Services Center, Charlottesville.

PICTURE CREDITS

BIBLIOGRAPHY

"Alcohol and Caffeine: Effect on Inferred Visual Dreaming." *Science,* June 14, 1963.

Ali, A. Yusuf, *The Holy Quran.* Brentwood, Md.: Amana, 1983.

Alley, Ronald, *Portrait of a Primitive: The Art of Henri Rousseau.* New York: E. P. Dutton, 1978.

Andrae, Tor, *Mohammed: The Man and His Faith.* Transl. by Theophil Menzel. New York: Harper & Row, 1960.

Aserinsky, Eugene, and Nathaniel Kleitman:
  "A Motility Cycle in Sleeping Infants as Manifested by Ocular and Gross Bodily Activity." *Journal of Applied Physiology,* July 1955.
  "Regularly Occurring Periods of Eye Motility, and Concomitant Phenomena, during Sleep." *Science,* September 4, 1953.

Baeyer, Hans Christian von, "A Dream Come True." *The Sciences,* January-February 1989.

Batten, Mary, "The Snoozing Zoo." *Science Digest,* July 1981.

de Becker, Raymond, *The Understanding of Dreams.* Transl. by Michael Heron. New York: Hawthorn Books, 1968.

Beradt, Charlotte, *The Third Reich of Dreams.* Transl. by Adriane Gottwald. Chicago, Ill.: Quadrangle Books, 1968.

Bertini, M., Helen B. Lewis, and Herman A. Witkin, "Some

Preliminary Observations with an Experimental Procedure for the Study of Hypnagogic and Related Phenomena." In *Altered States of Consciousness,* ed. by Charles T. Tart. Garden City, N.Y.: Doubleday, 1972.

Beveridge, W. I. B., *The Art of Scientific Investigation.* New York: W. W. Norton, 1957.

Blackmore, Susan J., *Beyond the Body.* London: Heinemann, 1982.

Boss, Medard, *The Analysis of Dreams.* Transl. by Arnold J. Pomerans. New York: Philosophical Library,1958.

Bower, B., "Recurrent Dreams: Clues to Conflict." *Science News,* March 29, 1986.

Breton, André, *Manifestoes of Surrealism.* Transl. by Richard Seaver and Helen R. Lane. Ann Arbor, Mich.: University of Michigan Press, 1969.

Brown, Eugene M., ed., *Dreams, Visions & Prophecies of Don Bosco.* New Rochelle, N.Y.: Don Bosco Publications, 1986.

Budzynski, Thomas, "Tuning In on the Twilight Zone." *Psychology Today,* August 1977.

Campbell, Joseph, *The Hero with a Thousand Faces.* Princeton, N.J.: Princeton University Press, 1968.

Campbell, Joseph, with Bill Moyers, *The Power of Myth.* Ed. by Betty Sue Flowers. New York: Doubleday, 1988.

Capps, Benjamin, and the Editors of Time-Life Books, *The Indians* (The Old West series). New York: Time-Life Books, 1973.

Cartwright, Rosalind, "Affect and Dream Work from an Information Processing Point of View." *The Journal of Mind and Behavior,* spring-summer 1986.

"Cave Men." *Time,* July 18, 1938.

Cavendish, Richard, ed., *Man, Myth & Magic.* New York: Marshall Cavendish, 1983.

Chagall, Marc, *Chagall by Chagall.* Ed. by Charles Sorlier, transl. by John Shepley. New York: Harry N. Abrams, 1979.

Cherry, Laurence, "Sleep's Biggest Riddle." *Science Digest,* July 1981.

Chittick, William C., *The Sufi Path of Love.* Albany: State University of New York Press, 1983.

Clark, Ronald W., *Freud: The Man and the Cause.* New York: Random House, 1980.

Clift, Jean Dalby, and Wallace B. Clift, *Symbols of Transformation in Dreams.* New York: Crossroad, 1984.

Coleman, Richard M., *Wide Awake at 3:00 A.M.: By Choice or by Chance?* New York: W. H. Freeman, 1986.

Colligan, Douglas, "Lucid Dreams." *Omni,* March 1982.

Compton, Susan, *Chagall.* New York: Harry N. Abrams, 1985.

Coxhead, David, and Susan Hiller, *Dreams: Visions of the Night.* New York: Crossroad, 1976.

Crick, Francis, and Graeme Mitchison, "REM Sleep and Neural Nets." *The Journal of Mind and Behavior,* spring-summer 1986.

de la Croix, Horst, and Richard G. Tansey, eds., *Gardner's Art through the Ages.* New York: Harcourt Brace Jovanovich, 1975.

Dee, Nerys, *Your Dreams & What They Mean.* Wellingborough, Northamptonshire, England: Aquarian Press, 1984.

Delaney, Gayle M. V., *Living Your Dreams.* San Francisco: Harper & Row, 1988.

De Martino, Manfred F., "Sex Differences in the Dreams of Southern College Students." *Journal of Clinical Psychology,* April 1953.

Dement, William C.:
"The Effect of Dream Deprivation." *Science,* June 10, 1960.

Some Must Watch while Some Must Sleep. San Francisco: San Francisco Book Company, 1976.

Descharnes, Robert, *Salvador Dali.* Transl. by Eleanor R. Morse. New York: Harry N. Abrams, 1976.

Ditlea, Steve, "The Dream Machine." *Omni,* October 1987.

Dodge, Christopher H., and Eugenia Lamont, "Sleep Learning in the USSR." Library of Congress, Aerospace Technology Division, report 68.91-108-6. Washington, D.C.: February 7, 1969.

Domhoff, G. William, *The Mystique of Dreams.* Berkeley: University of California Press, 1985.

Donn, Linda, *Freud and Jung.* New York: Charles Scribner's Sons, 1988.

Dunne, J. W., *An Experiment with Time.* London: Faber and Faber, 1934.

Evans, Christopher, *Landscapes of the Night.* Ed. by Peter Evans. New York: Viking Press, 1983.

Fagan, Joen, and Irma Lee Shepherd, eds., *Gestalt Therapy Now.* New York: Harper & Row, 1970.

Faraday, Ann, *The Dream Game.* London: Temple Smith, 1975.

Feinstein, David, and Stanley Krippner, *Personal Mythology.* Los Angeles: Jeremy P. Tarcher, 1988.

Fellini, Federico:
Fellini on Fellini. Ed. by Anna Keel and Christian Strich, transl. by Isabel Quigly. London: Eyre Methuen, 1976.
Juliet of the Spirits. Ed. by Tullio Kezich, transl. by Howard Greenfeld. New York: Ballantine Books, 1966.

Freemon, Frank R., *Sleep Research.* Springfield, Ill.: Charles C. Thomas, 1972.

Freud, Ernst, Lucie Freud, and Ilse Grubrich-Simitis, eds., *Freud.* Transl. by Christine Trollope. New York: Harcourt Brace Jovanovich, 1978.

Freud, Sigmund:
The Interpretation of Dreams. Transl. and ed. by James Strachey. London: George Allen & Unwin, 1954.
On Dreams. Transl. by James Strachey. New York: W. W. Norton, 1980.

Furst, Jill L., *North American Indian Art.* New York: Rizzoli, 1982.

Gackenbach, Jayne I.:
"Lucid Dreaming." In *Sleep Research,* ed. by Michael Chase, Daniel F. Kripke, and Pat L. Walter. Vol. 10. San Francisco: University of California, Brain Research Institute, 1981.
"A Survey of Considerations for Inducing Conscious Awareness of Dreaming while Dreaming." *Imagination, Cognition and Personality,* Vol. 5, No. 1, 1985-1986.

Galvin, Ruth Mehrtens, "Control of Dreams May Be Possible for a Resolute Few." Washington, D.C.: *Smithsonian,* August 1982.

Garfias, Robert, "The Role of Dreams and Spirit Possession in the *Mbira Dza Vadzimu* Music of the Shona People of Zimbabwe." *Journal of Altered States of Consciousness,* Vol. 5, No. 3, 1979-1980.

Garfield, Patricia L., *Creative Dreaming.* New York: Ballantine Books, 1974.

Gaunt, William, *The Surrealists.* New York: G. P. Putnam's Sons, 1972.

Gay, Peter, *Freud.* New York: W. W. Norton, 1988.

Giesler, Patric, "Lucid OBEs." *Parapsychology Review,* September-October 1986.

Glassé, Cyril, *The Concise Encyclopedia of Islam.* San Francisco: Harper & Row, 1989.

Glassman, Carl, "Sleep On It." *Science Digest,* July 1981.

Goldwater, Robert, *Space and Dream.* New York: Walker, 1967.

Griffin, Richard, *Typical Dreams.* University of Kentucky dissertation, 1950.

Grisell, Ronald, *Sufism.* Berkeley, Calif.: Ross Books, 1983.

Gutheil, Emil A.:
The Handbook of Dream Analysis. New York: Liveright, 1951.
The Language of the Dream. New York: Macmillan, 1939.

Hadfield, J. A., *Dreams and Nightmares.* Harmondsworth, Middlesex, England: Penguin Books, 1954.

Hall, Calvin S., "Wagnerian Dreams." *Psychology Today,* January 1983.

Hall, Calvin S., and Gardner Lindzey, *Theories of Personality.* New York: John Wiley & Sons, 1970.

Hall, James A., M.D., *Clinical Uses of Dreams.* New York: Grune & Stratton, 1977.

Harris, Irving D.:
"Characterological Significance of the Typical Anxiety Dreams." *Psychiatry,* August 1951.
"Observations concerning Typical Anxiety Dreams." *Psychiatry,* August 1948.

Hartmann, Ernest L., *The Functions of Sleep.* New Haven, Conn.: Yale University Press, 1973.

Hartmann, Ernest L., et al., "Who Has Nightmares?" In *Sleep Research,* ed. by Michael H. Chase, Daniel F. Kripke, and Pat L. Walter. Vol. 10. San Francisco: University of California, Brain Research Institute, 1981.

Haskell, Robert E., "Cognitive Psychology and Dream Research." *The Journal of Mind and Behavior,* spring-summer 1986.

Headrick, Mary F., "Dream-Level Therapy." *Journal of Counseling and Development,* November 1985.

Hearne, Keith M. T.:
"An Automated Technique for Studying Psi in Home 'Lucid' Dreams." *Journal of the Society for Psychical Research,* June 1982.
"A Dream-Telepathy Study Using a Home 'Dream Machine.'" *Journal of the Society for Psychical Research,* April 1987.
"The Effect on the Subject (in Waking, SWS and REM States) of Electric Shocks to the Agent." *Journal of the Society for Psychical Research,* June 1981.
"'Lucid' Dreams and ESP." *Journal of the Society for Psychical Research,* February 1981.
"An Ostensible Precognition of the Accidental Sinking of H. M. Submarine *Artemis* in 1971." *Journal of the Society of Psychical Research,* June 1982.
"An Ostensible Precognition Using a 'Dream-Machine.'" *Journal of the Society for Psychical Research,* February 1985.
"Three Cases of Ostensible Precognition from a Single Percipient." *Journal of the Society for Psychical Research,* June 1982.
Visions of the Future. Wellingborough, Northamptonshire, England: Aquarian Press, 1989.

Highwater, Jamake:
The Primal Mind: Vision and Reality in Indian America. New York: New American Library, 1981.
Ritual of the Wind. Toronto: Methuen, 1984.

History of Modern Art. Englewood Cliffs, N.J.: Prentice-Hall, 1977.

Hobson, J. Allan:
The Dreaming Brain. New York: Basic Books, 1988.
Sleep. New York: Scientific American Library, 1989.

Hobson, J. Allan, and Robert W. McCarley, M.D., "The Brain as a Dream State Generator." *The American Journal of Psychiatry,* December 1977.

Holroyd, Stuart, *Dream Worlds.* London: Aldus Books,

1976.

Hudson, Liam, *Night Life.* New York: St. Martin's Press, 1985.

Ibn Hisham, 'Abd al-Malik, ed. and transl., *The Life of Muhammad.* London: Oxford University Press, 1955.

Inglis, Brian:
  The Hidden Power. London: Jonathan Cape, 1986.
  The Power of Dreams. London: Collins Publishing Group, 1987.
  "Inner Space." *Science Digest,* July 1981.

Jacobi, Jolande, *Complex/Archetype/Symbol in the Psychology of C. G. Jung.* London: Routledge & Kegan Paul, 1959.

Jaffé, Aniela, ed., *C. G. Jung: Word and Image.* Transl. by Krishna Winston. Princeton, N.J.: Princeton University Press, 1979.

Jouvet, Michael, "The States of Sleep." In *Progress in Psychobiology* (Readings from *Scientific American*). San Francisco: W. H. Freeman, 1976.

Jung, C. G.:
  The Archetypes and the Collective Unconscious. Transl. by R. F. C. Hull. Princeton, N.J.: Princeton University Press, 1969.
  Mandala Symbolism. Ed. by Herbert Read, Michael Fordham, and Gerhard Adler. Princeton, N.J.: Princeton University Press, 1972.
  Memories, Dreams, Reflections. Ed. by Aniela Jaffé, transl. by Richard Winston and Clara Winston. New York: Random House, 1963.

Jung, Carl G., et al., *Man and His Symbols.* New York: Doubleday, 1964.

Kagan, Fred, ed., *Hypnotics.* New York: Spectrum Publications, 1975.

Kelsey, Morton T., *Dreams: The Dark Speech of the Spirit.* Garden City, N.Y.: Doubleday, 1968.

Kleitman, Nathaniel, *Sleep and Wakefulness.* Chicago: University of Chicago, 1963.

Kracke, Waud, "Myths in Dreams, Thought in Images." In *Dreaming: Anthropological and Psychological Interpretations,* ed. by Barbara Tedlock. Cambridge, England: Cambridge University Press, 1987.

Krippner, Stanley:
  "Dreams and the Development of a Personal Mythology." *The Journal of Mind and Behavior,* spring-summer 1986.
  Human Possibilities. Garden City, N.J.: Doubleday, 1980.

Krippner, Stanley, and Joseph Dillard, *Dreamworking.* Buffalo, N.Y.: Bearly Limited, 1988.

Krüll, Marianne, *Freud and His Father.* Transl. by Arnold J. Pomerans. New York: W. W. Norton, 1986.

LaBerge, Stephen:
  Lucid Dreaming. Los Angeles: Jeremy P. Tarcher, 1985.
  "Lucid Dreaming: Directing the Action as It Happens." *Psychology Today,* January 1981.
  "Lucid Dreaming in Western Literature." In *Conscious Mind, Sleeping Brain,* ed. by Jayne Gackenbach and Stephen LaBerge. New York: Plenum Press, 1988.

LaBerge, Stephen, and Jayne Gackenbach, "Lucid Dreaming." In *Handbook of States of Consciousness,* ed. by Benjamin B. Wolman and Montague Ullman. New York: Van Nostrand Reinhold, 1986.

Lamberg, Lynne:
  The American Medical Association Guide to Better Sleep. New York: Random House, 1984.
  "Night Pilot." *Psychology Today,* July-August 1988.

Lessa, William A., and Evon Z. Vogt, *Reader in Comparative Religion.* New York: Harper & Row, 1965.

Lincoln, Jackson Steward, *The Dream in Primitive Cultures.* New York: Johnson Reprint, 1970.

Lindskoog, Kathryn, *The Gift of Dreams: A Christian View.* San Francisco: Harper & Row, 1979.

Long, Michael E., "What Is This Thing Called Sleep?" *National Geographic,* December 1987.

McDonald, Margaret C., "The Dream Debate: Freud vs. Neurophysiology." *Science News,* June 13, 1981.

McDonald, Phoebe, *Dreams: Night Language of the Soul.* Baton Rouge, La.: Mosaic Books, 1987.

MacKenzie, Norman, *Dreams and Dreaming.* New York: Vanguard Press, 1965.

Mahoney, Maria F., *The Meaning in Dreams and Dreaming.* New York: Citadel Press, 1966.

Mattoon, Mary Ann, *Applied Dream Analysis.* New York: John Wiley & Sons, 1978.

Mavromatis, Andreas, *Hypnagogia.* London: Routledge & Kegan Paul, 1987.

Melnechuk, Theodore, "The Dream Machine." *Psychology Today,* November 1983.

Michaud, Joseph Fr., *Michaud's History of Mysore.* Transl. by V. K. Raman Menon. New Delhi: Asian Educational Services, 1985.

Miller, Laurence, "REM Sleep: Pilot Light of the Mind?" *Psychology Today,* September 1987.

Miller, Richard, transl., *Henri Rousseau* (exhibition catalog). New York: The Museum of Modern Art, 1985.

The Miraculous Journey of Mahomet: Miraj Nameh. Intro. and comment. by Marie-Rose Séguy. London: Scolar Press, 1977.

Moore, Michael C., and Lynda J. Moore, *The Complete Handbook of Holistic Health.* Englewood Cliffs, N.J.: Prentice-Hall, 1983.

Morris, Jill, *The Dream Workbook.* New York: Fawcett Crest, 1985.

Murchie, Guy, "Dreams: Do They Ever Stop? Can They See the Future?" *Science Digest,* April 1980.

Nigosian, Solomon A., *Islam.* Wellington, Northhampton-shire, England: Aquarian Press, 1987.

O'Flaherty, Wendy Doniger, *Dreams, Illusion and Other Realities.* Chicago: University of Chicago Press, 1984.

Ong, Roberto K., *The Interpretation of Dreams in Ancient China.* Hagen, German Democratic Republic: Bochum, 1985.

Painters of the Mind's Eye: Belgian Symbolists and Surrealists (exhibition catalog). New York: The New York Cultural Center, 1975.

Perls, Frederick S., *Gestalt Therapy Verbatim.* Comp. and ed. by John O. Stevens. New York: Bantam Books, 1959.

Petric, Vlada, *Film & Dreams: An Approach to Bergman.* South Salem, N.Y.: Redgrave, 1981.

Playfair, Guy Lyon, "Koestler, Mann and Schopenhauer." *Journal of the Society for Psychical Research,* October 1984.

Raising a Happy Child, by the Editors of Time-Life Books (The Successful Parenting series). Alexandria, Va.: Time-Life Books, 1986.

The Rand McNally Atlas of the Body and Mind. New York: Rand McNally, 1976.

Rubin, F., *Learning and Sleep.* Bristol, England: John Wright & Sons, 1971.

Ryback, David, and Letitia Sweitzer, *Dreams That Come True.* New York: Doubleday, 1988.

Sebba, Gregor, *The Dream of Descartes.* Ed. by Richard A. Watson. Carbondale, Ill.: Southern Illinois University Press, 1987.

Sehulster, Jerome R., "The Role of Altered States of Con-

sciousness in the Life, Theater, and Theories of Richard Wagner." *Journal of Altered States of Consciousness,* Vol. 5, No. 3, 1979-1980.

Sharma, Jagdish P., and Lee Siegel, *Dream-Symbolism in the Sramanic Tradition.* Calcutta: Firma KLM Private Ltd., 1980.

Shulman, Sandra, *Dreams.* London: Macdonald Unit 75, 1970.

Skogemann, P., "Chuang Tzu and the Butterfly Dream." *Journal of Analytical Psychology,* January 1986.

Snyder, Thomas J., and Jayne Gackenbach, "Individual Differences Associated with Lucid Dreaming." In *Conscious Mind, Sleeping Brain,* ed. by Jayne Gackenbach and Stephen LaBerge. New York: Plenum Press, 1988.

Soby, James Thrall, *Salvador Dali* (exhibition catalog). New York: The Museum of Modern Art, 1941.

Starker, Steven, *Fantastic Thought.* Englewood Cliffs, N.J.: Prentice-Hall, 1982.

Steene, Birgitta, ed., *Focus on The Seventh Seal.* Englewood Cliffs, N.J.: Prentice-Hall, 1972.

Stevens, Anthony, *Archetypes.* New York: Quill, 1983.

Stevens, William Oliver, *The Mystery of Dreams.* New York: Dodd, Mead, 1949.

Stewart, Desmond, and the Editors of Time-Life Books, *Early Islam* (The Great Ages of Man series). New York: Time-Life Books, 1967.

Storr, Anthony, *Solitude: A Return to the Self.* New York: Ballantine Books, 1988.

Swerdloff, Alissa, "The Body's Busy Night Shift." *Science Digest,* July 1981.

Tart, Charles T., ed., *Altered States of Consciousness.* Garden City, N.Y.: Doubleday, 1972.

Tedlock, Barbara, "Quiché Maya Dream Interpretation." *Ethos,* winter 1981.

Tedlock, Barbara, ed., *Dreaming: Anthropological and Psychological Interpretations.* Cambridge: Cambridge University Press, 1987.

Thurston, Mark, *Dreams.* San Francisco: Harper & Row, 1988.

Torczyner, Harry, *Magritte: Ideas and Images.* Transl. by Richard Miller. New York: Harry N. Abrams, 1977.

Toufexis, Anastasia, "Heavy Traffic on the Royal Road." *Time,* October 12, 1987.

Ullman, Montague, "Vigilance Theory and Psi." *The Journal of the American Society for Psychical Research,* October 1986.

Ullman, Montague, Stanley Krippner, and Alan Vaughan, *Dream Telepathy.* Jefferson, N.C.: McFarland, 1989.

Ullman, Montague, and Claire Limmer, *The Variety of Dream Experience.* New York: Continuum, 1987.

Ullman, Montague, and Edward F. Storm, "Dreaming and the Dream." *The Journal of Mind and Behavior,* spring-summer 1986.

Ullman, Montague, and Nan Zimmerman, *Working with Dreams.* Los Angeles: Jeremy P. Tarcher, 1979.

Underhill, Ruth M., *Red Man's Religion.* Chicago: University of Chicago Press, 1965.

Vogel, Virgil J., *American Indian Medicine.* New York: Ballantine Books, 1970.

Wagner, Cosima, *Cosima Wagner's Diaries: Volume I, 1869-1877.* Ed. by Martin Gregor-Dellin and Dietrich Mack, transl. by Geoffrey Skelton. New York: Harcourt Brace Jovanovich, 1976.

Wagner, Richard, *My Life.* Ed. by Mary Whittall, transl. by Andrew Gray. Cambridge: Cambridge University Press, 1983.

Wallach, Leah, "Recurring Dreams." *Omni,* February 1987.

Wehr, Gerhard, *Jung*. Boston: Shambhala, 1988.

Wernick, Robert, "From Out of the Past Come Thundering Hoofbeats of the Demon 'Nightmare.'" *Smithsonian*, March 1989.

Williams, Strephon Kaplan, *The Dreamwork Manual*. Berkeley, Calif.: Journey Press, 1985.

Winget, Carolyn, and Milton Kramer, *Dimensions of Dreams*. Gainesville, Fla.: University Presses of Florida, 1979.

Wolff, Werner, *The Mirror of Conscience*. New York: Grune & Stratton, 1952.

Wolman, Benjamin, ed., *Handbook of Dreams*. New York: Van Nostrand Reinhold, 1979.

Wolman, Benjamin B., and Montague Ullman, eds., *Handbook of States of Consciousness*. New York: Van Nostrand Reinhold, 1986.

"You Need Mental *Unrest* while You Sleep." *Life*, May 20, 1966.

INDEX

Time-Life Books Inc.
is a wholly owned subsidiary of
THE TIME INC. BOOK COMPANY

President and Chief Executive Officer: Kelso F. Sutton
President, Time Inc. Books Direct: Christopher T. Linen

TIME-LIFE BOOKS INC.

EDITOR: George Constable
Executive Editor: Ellen Phillips
Director of Design: Louis Klein
Director of Editorial Resources: Phyllis K. Wise
Editorial Board: Russell B. Adams, Jr., Dale M. Brown,
Roberta Conlan, Thomas H. Flaherty, Lee Hassig, Donia
Ann Steele, Rosalind Stubenberg
Director of Photography and Research: John Conrad Weiser

PRESIDENT: John M. Fahey, Jr.
Senior Vice Presidents: Robert M. DeSena, James L. Mercer,
Paul R. Stewart, Curtis G. Viebranz, Joseph J. Ward
Vice Presidents: Stephen L. Bair, Bonita L. Boezeman,
Stephen L. Goldstein, Juanita T. James, Andrew P. Kaplan,
Trevor Lunn, Susan J. Maruyama, Robert H. Smith
Supervisor of Quality Control: James King

PUBLISHER: Joseph J. Ward

Editorial Operations
Copy Chief: Diane Ullius
Production: Celia Beattie
Library: Louise D. Forstall
Computer Composition: Gordon E. Buck (Manager),
Deborah G. Tait, Monika D. Thayer, Janet Barnes Syring,
Lillian Daniels

Library of Congress Cataloging in Publication Data
Dreams and dreaming / by the editors of Time-Life Books.
p.   cm. — (Mysteries of the unknown.)
Includes bibliographical references.
ISBN 0-8094-6388-1. ISBN 0-8094-6389-X (lib. bdg.)
1. Dreams.   I. Time-Life Books.   II. Series.
BF1078.D73 1990   89-20272
154.6'3—dc20   CIP

MYSTERIES OF THE UNKNOWN

SERIES DIRECTOR: Jim Hicks
Series Administrator: Myrna Traylor-Herndon
Designers: Tom Huestis, Susan K. White

Editorial Staff for *Dreams and Dreaming*
Associate Editors: Sara Schneidman (pictures), Janet Cave
(text)
Text Editor: Robert A. Doyle
Researchers: Sarah D. Ince, Christian D. Kinney, Stephanie
Lewis, Philip M. Murphy
Staff Writers: Marfé Ferguson Delano, Margery A. duMond
Assistant Designer: Susan M. Gibas
Copy Coordinators: Mary Beth Oelkers-Keegan,
Jarelle S. Stein, Colette Stockum
Picture Coordinator: Katherine Griffin
Editorial Assistant: Donna Fountain

Special Contributors: Lesley Coleman, Christine Hinze
(London, picture research); Susan Yang K. Chew (lead
research); Patti H. Cass, Denise Dersin, Mark Galan,
Cornelia M. Piper, Mary E. Rose (research); Sarah Brash,
George Daniels, Lydia Preston Hicks, Robert A. Kiener,
Philip Mandelkorn, Wendy Murphy, Susan S. Perry, Peter
W. Pocock, Michael Pousner, Bryce S. Walker (text); John
Drummond (design); Hazel Blumberg-McKee (index)

Correspondents: Elisabeth Kraemer-Singh (Bonn), Christina
Lieberman (New York), Maria Vincenza Aloisi (Paris), Ann
Natanson (Rome).
Valuable assistance was also provided by Mirka Gondicas
(Athens); Angelika Lemmer (Bonn); Robert Kroon
(Geneva); Judy Aspinall (London); Simmi Dhanda, Deepak
Puri (New Delhi); Elizabeth Brown (New York); Ann Wise
(Rome).

Consultants:

Marcello Truzzi, professor of sociology at Eastern Michigan University, is also director of the Center for Scientific Anomalies Research (CSAR) and editor of its journal, the *Zetetic Scholar.* Dr. Truzzi, who considers himself a "constructive skeptic" with regard to claims of the paranormal, works through the CSAR to produce dialogues between critics and proponents of unusual scientific claims.

Jerome S. Bernstein is a practicing clinical psychologist and Jungian analyst in Washington, D.C. He received a master's degree in clinical psychology from George Washington University and is a graduate of the C. G. Jung Institute of New York. Dr. Bernstein, who is president of the C. G. Jung Analysts Association of the Greater Washington Metropolitan Area, has published several articles on psychology and politics.

Stanley Krippner is professor of psychology and director of the Center for Consciousness Studies at Saybrook Institute in San Francisco. Previously, he served as director of the Dream Laboratory at Maimonides Medical Center in Brooklyn. Dr. Krippner, who holds a Ph.D. in educational psychology from Northwestern University, has coauthored several books, including *Dream Telepathy: Experiments in Nocturnal ESP,* with Montague Ullman and Alan Vaughan, and *Dreamworking: How to Use Your Dreams for Creative Problem-Solving,* with Joseph Dillard.

Other Publications:

TIME-LIFE LIBRARY OF CURIOUS AND UNUSUAL FACTS
AMERICAN COUNTRY
VOYAGE THROUGH THE UNIVERSE
THE THIRD REICH
THE TIME-LIFE GARDENER'S GUIDE
TIME FRAME
FIX IT YOURSELF
FITNESS, HEALTH & NUTRITION
SUCCESSFUL PARENTING
HEALTHY HOME COOKING
UNDERSTANDING COMPUTERS
LIBRARY OF NATIONS
THE ENCHANTED WORLD
THE KODAK LIBRARY OF CREATIVE PHOTOGRAPHY
GREAT MEALS IN MINUTES
THE CIVIL WAR
PLANET EARTH
COLLECTOR'S LIBRARY OF THE CIVIL WAR
THE EPIC OF FLIGHT
THE GOOD COOK
WORLD WAR II
HOME REPAIR AND IMPROVEMENT
THE OLD WEST

For information on and a full description of any of the Time-Life Books series listed above, please call 1-800-621-7026 or write:
Reader Information
Time-Life Customer Service
P.O. Box C-32068
Richmond, Virginia 23261-2068

This volume is one of a series that examines the history and nature of seemingly paranormal phenomena. Other books in the series include: